Foreign Policy and
Economic Dependence

Foreign Policy and Economic Dependence

BY NEIL R. RICHARDSON

University of Texas Press   Austin & London

To the memory of my father,
John S. Richardson

Library of Congress Cataloging in Publication Data

Richardson, Neil R.   1944–
    Foreign policy and economic dependence.

    Includes bibliographical references and index.
    1. Underdeveloped areas—Economic policy.
2. Underdeveloped areas—Foreign relations. 3. International
economic relations. I. Title.
HC59.7.R49   338.9′009172′4   78-6451
ISBN 0-292-72425-X

Contents

Figures

Tables

Acknowledgments

I have accumulated many debts in writing this book and would like to acknowledge at least those who have directly contributed to its completion. At the same time, and after brief reflection, I realize that conventional disclaimers are only fair. Thus, I want to absolve these people of any responsibility for errors and weaknesses that remain despite their considerable help.

Thanks are due to Bruce Buchanan, Larry Dodd, Wilfried Prewo, Karl Schmitt, Norman Schofield, and Harrison Wagner for reading several chapters apiece. Each of them has offered numerous suggestions, critical, probing questions, and, simultaneously, moral support. James Lee Ray and Eugene R. Wittkopf read the entire manuscript with care, providing extensive and insightful commentaries of great value to the final revision.

On several occasions, I have called on Calvin P. Blair for assistance in attempts to overcome the intractability of valid data sources and measurement procedures in cross-national economic estimates. His resourcefulness has appreciably benefited the project. Carol O'Day has assisted with data analyses during the revision process, and has performed most ably under strict time constraints. Bill Moore has executed the lion's share of the data manipulations, bringing to them much-appreciated technical competence in econometric techniques and, importantly, enthusiasm.

I am also very grateful for financial support from the World Order Studies program and the University Research Institute, both of the University of Texas at Austin. The former made available a grant to cover a substantial share of my computer costs. The latter provided some funds for computer work and manuscript preparation. Most significantly, the Institute also granted me a Summer Research Award in 1976, a crucial time.

At the University of Texas Press, Barbara Burnham has guided the manuscript to its bound incarnation with skill and dispatch. Alison Heinemann has carefully edited the copy. Both of them have been a pleasure to work with. Concurrent with their efforts have been those of several staff members in the Department of Government who, as manuscript typists, are nonetheless willing to remain on good terms with me.

My ultimate safe harbor is Jane, who defines the many facets of friendship. She might protest, but I shall always be in her debt.

N. R.

Foreign Policy and
Economic Dependence

Chapter 1
Introduction

The nations of the world come in all sizes, several colors, and scores of languages. They also differ greatly in material wealth, literacy, birth rates, and politics. Nevertheless, they hold in common a faith in the virtues of "national development." Developed countries pride themselves on their achievements, while less-developed countries envy and emulate the developed ones.

National development, however, is one of those phrases that mean different things to different people. For example, some would first associate with national development the sense of belonging together that is often called nationalism. Others would immediately think of large-scale educational and health services to improve the welfare of a country's people. Political stability is likewise considered by many to be a sign of national development. But, for them and many others, national development is also linked to the society's economic system. Whether seen as clusters of smokestacks in dirty cities, as a favorable balance of foreign trade, or as food on the tables of the populace, national development is most commonly cast in economic images.

This worldwide pursuit of national development has coincided with the creation of technologies that, since the second world war, have greatly contributed to the growth of international transactions.[1] Whether one looks at international commerce, tourist traffic, mail flows, or diplomatic exchanges, the conclusion is inescapable that national societies are increasingly exposed to contacts with their environments. Moreover, the coincidence of these transactions with the advent of so many new, development-conscious, sovereign states is frequently put in causal form: transactions between developed and underdeveloped societies have led to the universal adoption of national development as a paramount goal.

This sort of linkage between developmental aspirations and international transactions draws attention to the great inequalities that exist among nations today. In some societies exists an abundance of material goods and services. But for much the larger share of humanity life offers instead an abundance of hunger, ignorance, and disease. It is only as they become aware of more attractive alternative life styles, via some contact with a part of the world different from their own, that the people of poor countries begin to push for more.

In a vastly unequal world, then, certain transactions between developed and less-developed countries are generally asymmetrical in their effects. The rich continue to thrive while the poor confront the perceived injustice of their unrelieved miseries. But unequal effects are not only to be found in the skewed distribution of wealth. Asymmetry exists, too, in the extent to which rich and poor countries rely on their external environment for the provision of whatever prosperity they may enjoy.

This last point brings to center stage questions about the meaning of "interdependence," a term that warrants some further elaboration. Interdependence between two entities can be defined as *mutual* dependence upon their transactions. In the words of Robert Keohane and Joseph Nye, "interdependence in world politics refers to situations characterized by reciprocal effects among countries or among actors in different countries." [2] In principle, these "effects" may include benefits that accrue to the participants as a result of their relationship. Interdependence will always entail some cost, however, since each participant's autonomy is constrained by its dependence. Foreign trade is a good example of international interdependence featuring both costs and benefits. The joint decision of two countries, A and B, to exchange goods and services with each other is presumably based on determinations that A can acquire from B something that A either cannot provide for itself or at least can provide for itself only at greater cost. The same can be said for B's decision to buy from A. Once A and B have established their trade relationship, both become dependent on its continuation, hence interdependent. In other words, each country is dependent on the other for certain provisions and is thereby dependent on the other's renewed decisions to supply something of value.

This interdependence framework is of interest to students of world politics in part because it draws attention to the opportunities that actors may have to use their interdependence to alter the behavior of their partners in those relationships. Such *political* opportunities arise only if the interdependence is *a*symmetrical. If, for example, country A gains more from its trade with B than the other way around, B would appear to have less to lose by interrupting that trade than would A. This situation would therefore seem to provide B with an opportunity to influence the behavior of A, whether with respect to the trade relationship itself or some other issue of interest to B.

On the other hand, Keohane and Nye suggest that there are actually two dimensions to the dependence that each party will experience.[3] Furthermore, each dimension must be assessed before one can determine whether there is, on balance, a political advantage for any participant. The first facet of a country's dependence is its *sensitivity* to change brought about by the decision of a partner. Sensitivity pertains to the resultant costs incurred by the target before it can adjust to the change in its international environment. *Vulnerability*, their second dimension of dependence, refers to the longer-term costs suffered by the target even after it has adjusted its policies to the new circumstances as best it can.

Of the two, vulnerability is thought to be the more important to an understanding of the politics of asymmetrical interdependence. Sensitivity, after all, is based only on short-run costs. The United States may have appeared at one time to be dependent on sugar imports from Cuba. Indeed, when those imports were shut off, the U.S. suffered sensitivity costs. But U.S. demands for sugar were rather easily met by adjustment policies, including subsidized domestic production as well as recourse to other foreign suppliers. Long-run vulnerability costs were, in this case, quite low. Thus, U.S. dependence on Cuban sugar did not provide much political leverage for that Caribbean country despite the initial costs associated with cessation of trade.

This study examines economic and political relations between rich and poor countries where, many observers believe, asymmetrical interdependence most frequently occurs. Their suspicions are based on theoretical propositions and sketchy evidence. However, it should be noted at the outset that on at least one count this thesis rests on fairly solid footing: patterns of international economic transactions for both rich and poor countries tend to follow what Johan Galtung has aptly called "rank-dependent behavior."[4] This means that countries of high rank in an international hierarchy characteristically behave differently from countries lower in the pecking order. Thus, in the clear majority of their international economic transactions poor countries deal with rich countries rather than with other poor ones. Meanwhile, the rich nations interact more extensively with each other than with poor countries. Another indication of asymmetry in rich-poor relations is the demonstrated fact that, for a low-ranking (nonindustrial) country, the share of its gross national product in foreign trade tends to be much larger than the foreign trade sector of a high-ranking (industrial) country's annual economic activity.[5] Together, these discoveries establish a strong preliminary basis for the general statement that, ceteris paribus, in economic relationships between poor and rich countries the former are considerably more sensitive to the latter's decisions than the other way around.

Asymmetries in international economic relations are also of great interest to students of *dependencia*. Their writings reflect a clear marxist orientation, with heavy emphasis on transnational alliances of ruling elites in both rich and poor capitalist countries.[6] The self-interested and exploitative behavior of these elites is, in turn, said to explain several observable phenomena, including asymmetrical economic ties between rich and poor societies. Consider, for example, Dos Santos' oft-quoted definition: "By dependence we mean a situation in which the economy of certain countries is conditioned by the development and expansion of another economy to which the former is subjected. The relation of interdependence between two or more economies, and between these and world trade, assumes the form of dependence when some countries (the dominant ones) can expand and can be self-starting, while other countries (the dependent ones) can do this only as a reflection of that expansion, which can have either a positive or a negative effect on their immediate development."[7]

As *dependencia* scholars address the complementary motives of elites in (dominant) rich and (dependent) poor countries, their main concern is with the "distortions" in, or even the absence of, economic development in nonindustrial societies that is a result. At the same time, such matters invariably raise issues of international economic relations between dominant and dependent societies. Elites in both sets of countries are said to collaborate to the general detriment of dependent economies, and their decisions are reflected in the disproportionately large costs and/or small benefits attending the international economic transactions of dependencies. Finally, *dependencia* highlights not only the ingredients of external sensitivity plaguing poor economies, but also attempts to explain their long-run vulnerability to foreign domination.

Now, for a poor country that comes to be highly dependent on its economic transactions with a rich one, its politics may be importantly affected. In keeping with the assumption that politics and economics of rich-poor international relations are closely entwined, the present study will scrutinize both. But it is an understanding of the political behavior of a dependency, even more than of its economic dependence as such, that is the object of this book. Among the questions to be examined are: What sorts of economic transactions produce dependence in the first place? Under what conditions are they potentially most enslaving? What are the domestic political reactions to such asymmetrical ties? How does the government of a dependent nation try to strike a balance between the distasteful necessity of foreign ties and domestic pressures for genuine national self-determination? To what extent is such a government's foreign policy compromised by its economy's vulnerability to external manipulation?

As just implied, then, this is an examination of international political economy. It begins with the explicit premise that politics and economics are, in many settings, intimately associated. Indeed, it is assumed that international politics between mighty states and weak ones can only be understood by paying close attention to their economic relations at the same time. Although political economy embraces the notion that politics and economics are associated by reciprocal causation, each a determinant of the other, this study is particularly concerned with the one half of that general orientation which searches for political *consequences* of economics, rather than for political *causes* of them.[8]

The general orientation of this study is not novel, of course. But in the past few years, research on rich-poor political economy has been given new impetus by four developments. The first of these is the attack by poor countries on the terms of their trade with rich ones, articulated through the United Nations Conference on Trade and Development (UNCTAD), and more recently incorporated in appeals for a "New International Economic Order." The second and most visible development has been the smashing success of the Organization of Petroleum Exporting Countries (OPEC) on both economic and political fronts. The third has been the remarkable growth of the multinational corporation—economic production organized at such a high level that its activities transcend national regulation to the great consternation of poor countries' leaders. Finally, and galvanized by the ambitious *Limits to Growth* study,[9] there is now emerging some concerted thought about the political economy of food and population, forces of greatest pressure for the world's poorest societies. Indeed, so fundamental are these sorts of concerns that even the two superpowers show signs of waning preoccupation with their cold war.

If the political economy of relations between rich and poor states is experiencing a surge of attention for these reasons, their international relations also merit close study on more fundamental grounds.[10] For example, the poor countries of the world number more than two-thirds of the membership of the international system, yet their foreign policies have only very recently received much scholarly notice. If one scientific objective is to develop generalizations based on all classes of objects or events, then the foreign policies of poor countries deserve more attention than they have traditionally received. The oversight is all the more remarkable in light of the fact that from among this class of "weak" or "peripheral" states' foreign policies have sprung conflicts of global import, including those in Southeast Asia, Cuba, Southern Africa, and the Middle

East. The political economy of relations between rich and poor is a matter of profound importance whose day seems finally to have come.

But, whatever the reasons that these relations are now considered an important subject, even a fashionable one, interest in them follows a substantial tradition of thought on the origins and consequences of formal empire. And it is here, in studies of imperialism, that one finds an intersection of marxist and more orthodox analysts of political economy: far-flung empires governed by European metropoles are now history, having been dissolved almost completely in the past three decades. But the concept of dependence draws heavily from the *informal* control that remains as the legacy of poor countries' colonial experience. Thus, even in the absence now of formal political governance, the economic dependence of poor societies on the rich persists, with potent political implications. Marxists and neoclassical economists clearly disagree on the detailed workings of international economics between rich and poor. Indeed, descriptive terms often employed by marxists include "imperialism," "new imperialism," and "neocolonialism," while neoclassicists are more prone to refer to a "division of labor" and, more optimistically, "harmony of interests." Despite the differences these terms imply, these scholars largely concur on two broader themes: (1) economic transactions between rich and poor societies have asymmetrical effects; (2) these economic ties may have deep political repercussions within the poor polities. A third statement is consistent with the first two, but less frequently mentioned: (3) the political consequences of asymmetrical economic relations extend to the foreign policy behavior of poor countries. Together, these three assertions form the basis for this study.

There is perhaps no single term or phrase to describe these relations that will not be resisted by some because of its perceived emotive connotations. Accordingly, "dependence" has been selected for use in this study in hopes that it can be regarded as more neutral than the alternatives referred to above and because it is not so awkward as "asymmetrical interdependence." In any case, it is of course more important for the reader to reach judgment about the theoretical, empirical, and interpretive content of the following chapters independently of initial reactions to "dependence" or to any other of the more specific terms employed in the study.

It is also worth noting that a focus on international dependence, by whatever label, promotes two objectives of genuine intellectual merit. First, it serves as a common substantive focus for both marxists and nonmarxists. Only the most doctrinaire ideologue would deny the relevance of their meeting on common ground. Second, dependence is a concept that can and should bridge studies of national development and international relations. Here it is too often the case that scholars may pay lip service to the value of incorporating ideas from other domains into their own without seriously attempting to do so. Ideas of dependence compel this greater breadth, as well as the synergistic cross-fertilization of ideas the merger promises.

Accordingly, the following pages extract ideas about the political economy of dependence from marxists and nonmarxists whose work has dealt with at least some relevant aspects of national development and/or international relations. However fair and successful this distillation, it is not a complete synthesis, nor can it exhaust the theoretical possibilities that inhere in the admixture. Nowhere is this shortcoming more marked than in Chapter 2, where some central features of international economic dependence are reviewed. The failure there to develop a single and coherent theory of dependence is owed at least partly to the basic incompatibility of the (often untested) premises from which various commentators begin. The third chapter, even more speculative than the second, presents the bases for competing expectations about the effects of economic dependence upon the foreign policy behavior of elites in a country so constrained.

Thereafter follow two chapters describing and digesting data analysis that tests theoretical derivations from the preceding. It should come as no surprise that the results are not definitive. Instead, the interpretation must be qualified on two counts. First, the empirical materials are restricted to a particular set of countries and a limited frame of time. Hopefully, the choices of a U.S.-dominated group of countries taken for the years 1950 to 1973 have their own virtues when compared to alternate sets of countries and other time periods. The second type of qualification is more serious. Given the embryonic state of theoretical development alluded to earlier, the theory of dependence is overidentified; the results of this study help to narrow the range of explanations that are consistent with the evidence, but they cannot point to the one true path to theoretical closure. Sobered by these considerations, Chapter 6 briefly reconsiders the general character of dependence through the longer lenses of some broad issues of national development and international relations in a hierarchical world.

Chapter 2
International Economic Dependence

Economic transactions among countries take three principal forms—foreign trade, private investment, and foreign aid.[1] The International Monetary Fund will be included as a special case in the third category, which then subsumes monetary relations. The bulk of this chapter is devoted to these three economic phenomena with attention to their respective asymmetries in relations between rich and poor countries. A further effort is made to develop a coherent statement of dependence on trade, investment, and aid from a notably incomplete and scattered body of writings.

Before turning to these ideas, however, the discussion focuses on two additional premises to supplement the notion of influence already introduced. First, consistent with the idea of rank-dependent behavior applied to relations between rich and poor (as reviewed in the Introduction) is the simplifying assumption that asymmetrical international economics follow a pattern of "multiple bilateralism." In other words, the theoretical and empirical efforts undertaken here mirror the general historical pattern that poor countries' partners in international economics are rich countries rather than other poor countries. Although a simplification, this assumption seldom does serious violence to the facts. In the fields of foreign aid and foreign investment there is very little disparity between the assumption of bilateralism and reality. In foreign trade the gap is wider in some instances, but not compellingly so.

A second introductory comment concerns the psychology of dependence. Several students of dependence have asserted that such economically based influence need not explicitly include mention of asymmetrical vulnerabilities.[2] Instead, they say, the relevant decision-makers in a poor society have internalized at least a general awareness of their country's exposed position and treat decisions pertaining to their rich partners accordingly. The present study incorporates the assumption that elites in poor countries constantly take into account their economic dependence, with at least a general sense of what that condition implies regarding the availability of valued economic commodities.

To summarize these three assumptions, one could say that decision-makers in dependent countries value foreign-supplied economic goods and services that they almost exclusively receive at the discretion of a single, dominant partner, and that knowledge of this liability affects their behavior. On the other side of the coin, of course, decision-makers in dominant countries have predominant control over the availability of the economic goods and services that are highly valued by poor countries. These perspectives of elites in dominant and dependent countries are important to the mechanisms of dependence discussed below, and they will emerge even more explicitly in Chapter 3.

An Organizing Framework

Asymmetries in international economic relations invite a blend of "interdependence" ideas and those of *depen-*

dencia. The grounds for the merger are clearest if two points are kept in mind. First, the interdependence perspective emphasizes the importance of vulnerability to long-run costs (and the political leverage thereby afforded) in certain types of asymmetrical relationships. *Dependencia* theory can then be seen to add a second, temporal dimension to vulnerability as it highlights the perpetually subordinate role of poor, undiversified economies oriented toward serving the world capitalist system that entraps them. In short, *dependencia* scholars believe that poor economies are relegated to a semipermanent condition of underdevelopment, a condition that generally leaves them prey to what others call "vulnerability" in their economic transactions with rich countries.

The remainder of this chapter turns to a discussion of how trade, investment, and aid relations may result in poor countries' sensitivity and, especially, vulnerability. To this end, it is instructive to begin with a brief consideration of the pioneering work of Albert Hirschman some thirty-five years ago.[3] At that time, he began to develop a scheme of trade dominance by major powers, with empirical application to Nazi Germany's penetration into Eastern Europe. For some reason, perhaps because his book is not much concerned with Third World dependence, its ideas have not been explicitly incorporated into more recent treatments. Nonetheless, his framework shows clearly that he anticipated the outlines of contemporary analyses.

Hirschman's initial distinction is between two purposes that foreign trade may serve. On the one hand, the sale of exports pays for imports of valued goods from other countries; trade has a "supply effect." More germane to dependence, however, is the "power effect" of trade: "The power to interrupt commercial or financial relations with any country, considered as an attribute of national sovereignty, is the root cause of the influence or power position which a country acquires in other countries, just as it is the root cause of the 'dependence on trade.' "[4] Because A's decision to interrupt trade with B has negative supply effects for both partners, A can use threatened interruption as a political weapon only if B would suffer more from the stoppage than would A. In other words, the latent threat of stoppage attending the supply effect creates the opportunity for a power effect. A's dominance of B, he continues, can be divided into two analytic conditions. First, B must be extensively reliant on the world trade system, and, second, it must be difficult for B to shift its trade away from A toward alternative partners. In short, Hirschman was alert to both sensitivity and vulnerability dependence.

Indeed, his concluding prescriptions for successful trade dominance are in part organized around these two dimensions. To heighten a partner's potential short-run costs, he recommended that the dominant country trade with poor countries and increase their trade gains. Long-run cost prospects could be increased, he said, by trading with countries having low resource mobility and by encouraging them to specialize in export production for which there is little domestic demand. He added that it would be useful to create vested interests in trade within the business and elite communities of their societies.

This partial summary of Hirschman's recommendations amply shows the relevance of his study to present concerns. In the days of Hitler, of course, foreign investment operated on a small scale by today's standards, and foreign aid was virtually nonexistent. But it should also be pointed out that Hirschman's presentation is essentially static. There is no indication here that dominant-dependent relations, once established, may change or at least be forced to adapt to exogenous forces. In the surrounding text, however, he gives implicit recognition to processes of change as he notes that a dominant country's interests are served by discouraging industrialization in a dependent economy.

More recent studies of dependence often focus on economic development in less-developed societies, reflecting the subsequent primacy of developmental aspirations in poor countries. This chapter concludes with an expanded version of the Hirschman scheme that takes into account private investment and foreign aid as well as the matter of developmental change.

Trade Dependence

Foreign trade is broadly construed as a mutually beneficial enterprise. The origins of this assertion are in the well-known classical and neoclassical economics associated with Ricardo, Heckscher and Ohlin, Marshall, and numerous others.[5] The gains accruing to traders are based on "comparative advantages" particular to national economies that differ in their respective endowments of land, labor, and capital or in technology, time of industrialization, and so forth. In terms of opportunity costs of production, some countries find it relatively less expensive than others to produce grains. Other countries are well suited to produce minerals or manufactures instead. Because economies differ, each can efficiently arrange to produce certain goods for sale abroad, purchasing from other countries some of those goods which it is relatively ill suited to produce itself.

Benefits of trade based on comparative advantage are two. First, as an *im*porter of certain commodities, a country can buy those goods from abroad at a lower price (in terms of receipts from its exports) than it would pay if it were producing them for itself. The cheaper imports effectively increase national income by allowing consumers to purchase goods at a lower price. Second, as an *ex*porter of certain commodities, a country is channeling more of its productive resources into commodities for which it is a relatively efficient producer. Its excess production is sold abroad for proceeds that allow it, in turn, to pay for its imports.

The net result of different nations engaging in specialized production and trade is a division of labor among them. Classical economists essentially took for granted that a division of labor would create a harmony of interests. Each would stand to gain, but not at the expense of other trading nations. However, many observers no longer think that the international division of labor profits the poorer economies in the long run, even though it promotes international trade and the efficient use of the world's productive resources.[6]

The criticism of division of labor comes in two forms. Some hold that trade, operating in *benign* conformance with neoclassical economic theory, perpetuates the poverty of some members of the international economic system. Others go further by arguing that the inequalities are *consciously* exploited by the wealthy in trade with their poor partners. Critics are in greater agreement on the types of trade problems encountered by poor countries than they are regarding the locus of guilt. The problems most frequently identified are of three types: (1) trade has unequal effects on rich and poor countries; (2) primary goods exporters suffer from weaknesses that inhere in unprocessed goods markets; (3) the effects of tariffs discriminate against poor countries both because of the small size of their economies and their propensity to export primary goods.

UNEQUAL EFFECTS FOR RICH AND POOR ECONOMIES

The arguments for unequal benefits from trade are several. To begin, imagine that two countries, one rich and one poor, are following their comparative advantages to trade $500 million worth of goods to one another each year. The trade may be "equal," but its effects are not.

For the rich partner, the $500 million represents only a very small portion of its annual economic activity. But that same amount represents a much greater share of the poor partner's economy. The unequal effects of this difference take two forms. On the one hand, the poor country receives a larger share of its goods for home consumption at reduced, import prices than does the rich partner. This is to the poor country's advantage, of course, as long as the prices it must pay for its imports remain below those it would pay were it to produce the same goods at home. Second, and more important for a poor economy, a substantial share of its production of goods depends on sales to another country. For economic or noneconomic reasons the rich country might choose to curtail or even cease purchase of the poor country's export goods, and for a small, probably fragile, economy such a loss of sales could be ruinous. In short, the rich partner has much less to *gain or lose* from major changes in its foreign trade patterns than does the poor one; a poor country is much more trade dependent.[7]

Why, then, does the poor country trade abroad in the first place? Would it not be better off to end its dependence by ceasing trade with, at least, its rich partners? While this "solution" might have some momentary appeal, in fact a poor country is desperate to earn foreign exchange in order to buy abroad those commodities it does not and usually cannot produce, ranging from capital goods to luxury items.[8] These imports, of course, are more highly differentiated than the unprocessed goods the poor country sells abroad. Thus, the poor country compounds the vulnerability bred of its greater gains from trade by importing commodities for which identical substitutes from alternative suppliers are difficult or impossible to obtain. Not only are habits developed regarding preferences for consumer goods identified with certain brand names, but alternative replacement parts and services for capital goods are often unsatisfactory. In short, the poorer partner experiences greater trade gains and also faces greater adjustment difficulties should that trade be cut off.

A second view of the inequalities that result from the unfettered play of economic forces concerns the search for markets. From this perspective, firms seek ever-larger markets in order to increase production and thereby generate added profits. When national demand is met, the only potential for expansion is abroad via trade. This version of the theme is especially prominent in some writings on nineteenth-century imperialism.[9] One hundred years ago, the rich countries nearly monopolized the transportation necessary to expand markets by overseas trade. In consequence, it could be argued that rich countries were taking advantage of their wealth in their trade with poor societies.

Particularly with the rise of the giant corporation, though, the "larger markets" thesis today incorporates more commonly the principle of economies of scale. Thus, foreign trade penetration permits manufacturers greater profits by virtue both of larger volume of sales and of reductions in per-unit costs of production as volume increases.[10] Why is it that poor countries do not also seek economies of scale by overseas sales? Because, unlike rich countries, the poor ones do not specialize in capital-intensive, industrial goods production. And it is precisely these industries that can realize the greatest economies of scale. Accordingly, as rich trade with poor, the former can profit more from the market expansion that both experience as they export to the other a portion of their total production.[11]

But must poor countries remain poor? Or can they, too, industrialize to escape the misfortunes just described? On this matter of development the dependence literature dwells at considerable length. In so doing, it again devotes much of its attention to trade relations, which are characterized by the poor country's reliance on raw materials exports.

The implications of foreign trade for development in poor societies are said to hinge importantly on the characteristic division of labor between rich and poor. The latter commonly find their comparative advantages for trade in unprocessed goods and simple manufactures, including both foodstuffs and extractive products. These are commodities needed in large quantity by the industrial countries that, in turn, use these ingredients in the manufacture of highly processed goods. Here the poor countries are thought to encounter a difficulty. The world prices for primary goods are said to have been declining relative to those for manufactures since the second world war. That is, the exports of poor countries allegedly provide them a lower rate of purchasing power for needed imports than before; these countries suffer from "declining terms of trade."[12]

A second difficulty for primary goods exporters concerns another aspect of prices. Unprocessed goods, and in particular foodstuffs, have a history of fluctuating prices over time.[13] Such fluctuations make it especially difficult for poor countries to project their foreign exchange earnings from one fiscal year to the next. Therefore, it is not easy for them to plan their national budgets with confidence and security. Nevertheless, because they continue to have a comparative advantage in unprocessed goods, and because they also desperately need the foreign exchange earned from the sale of those goods, poor countries continue to specialize in primary goods production.

Reliance on primary goods exports is also deleterious to a poor country's economic development to the extent that these unprocessed goods dominate the domestic economy. These countries do not benefit from the "externalities" that accrue to societies engaged in industrial manufacturing.[14] That is, primary goods production is seldom accompanied by "spin-offs," those derivative economic activities that are themselves conducive to upgrading of labor skills, technological advances, and further capital accumulation. Galtung provides the hypothetical example of two countries exchanging tractors for crude oil: "In one nation the oil deposit may be at the water-front, and all that is needed is a derrick and some simple mooring facilities to pump the oil . . . to the country where it will provide energy to run, among other things, the tractor factories. In the other nation the effects may be extremely far-reaching due to the complexity of the product and the connectedness of the society."[15]

Because the colonial experience of these countries usually dictated an emphasis on the export sector, the primary goods distortion is a lingering legacy. To the attendant problems of declining terms of trade, price instability, and few spin-offs, poor economies must also add consideration of tariffs on trade.

TARIFF DISCRIMINATION

Most critics of such economic dependence do not regard the international division of labor as simply an artifact of the market place. Prominent in their writing are attacks on tariffs. The discriminatory effect of tariffs on prices can be described as unintentional, they concede, but one cannot be so charitable when considering the *structure* of tariffs now imposed on different types of commodities.

First, consider how tariffs work to the disadvantage of the small, poor economy in the world market. A poor country determined to industrialize might develop a strategy based on the following observation. Tariffs placed on its imports (and imports are largely manufactures from industrial countries) can serve two purposes: (1) tariffs provide additional revenue to the government; (2) by selective application, tariffs can protect "infant industries," new manufacturing facilities that must initially be protected from foreign competition because they have not yet achieved technical proficiency, economies of scale, and so forth.

But erecting tariffs poses a special problem for poor countries.[16] A poor economy is likely to constitute a very small share of world demand for the imports on which it has imposed tariffs. Therefore, its decision to raise domestic prices (by imposing tariffs) will not affect the world prices of those goods. However, the now-higher domestic prices of imports result in a lower real income for the populace. By contrast, a large, wealthy economy may be such a major buyer of world imports that its decision to impose tariffs has significantly different results. Once again, the tariffs raise the price that domestic consumers must pay. However, the reduced consumption of imports by the large economy will then tend to depress the world price of the goods in question, thereby penalizing the exporters. Thus, only the large economy can shift some of the costs of the tariff away from its domestic consumers onto the foreign suppliers.

Another problem with tariffs is related to the goal of protecting infant industries from more efficient overseas competitors. Setting aside the possibiilty of retaliatory tariffs for the moment, one can recognize that protective tariffs do offer poor countries some limited relief. Domestic industries can be nurtured, and if their purpose is to produce manufactures as substitutes for imported goods, they may be successful. One important result of import substitution, of course, is to reduce a poor country's need to earn foreign exchange with its exports. However, it should also be pointed out that the domestic market for manufactures is characteristically small simply because these goods, in themselves expensive to produce, will be even more costly because a domestic producer may not fully realize economies of scale in such a small market. In other words, the small home market tends to raise the price of the import substitutes, in turn reinforcing their low-volume, high-cost production.

Further, a manufacturer of import substitutes, once established at home, then faces formidable obstacles to successful entry into the world market.[17] As implied above, economies of scale that allow manufactured goods to be sold abroad at a price competitive with other world suppliers is difficult for the firm that begins with a small home market. Sales abroad also impose substantial overhead costs, including a trained sales force, a distribution network, and, for most types of products, a service/parts system. In sum, a poor-country strategy to enter the world market by combining selective tariffs with import substitution encounters high barriers.

The structure of tariffs further contributes to the perpetuation of poor countries' dependence on unprocessed exports.[18] The levels of import tariffs assessed by industrial countries correspond closely to the level of processing associated with commodity types. In his study of twenty-two "primary products" that enter into processing, Bela Balassa shows how dramatic the differences in tariff levels are, as shown in Table 1.[19] His figures indicate that, in trying to move up the scale of processing, a nonindustrial country at each step encounters increasing tariff barriers in the major world markets comprised of the industrial giants. The United States, for example, places no tariff on imported iron ore. But a 20 percent duty is levied against sewing needles.[20]

The percentages in the right-hand column attest to the fact that underdeveloped countries mainly export unprocessed goods. The tariff structure is not the sole cause of this export pattern, however. One rival or supplementary cause is the greater cost of transportation faced by many poor countries because they are so distant from the principal industrial buyers of their goods. Moreover, these countries have greater difficulties achieving economies of scale

Table 1. *Tariffs on Goods Imported from
Underdeveloped Countries*

Degree of Processing of Goods	Weighted Average Tariff Imposed:		Percentage Share in the Exports of Underdeveloped Countries
	Nominal[a]	Real[b]	
1	4.6	....	71.2
2	7.9	22.6	23.8
3	16.2	29.7	2.9
4	22.1	38.4	2.1

[a] In percentage of the export value.
[b] In percentage of the sales value.

in shipping. Shipping costs, in other words, may be very significant for unprocessed goods that commonly have a low value per ton in the first place.[21]

SUMMARY

To summarize the trade dependence thesis: foreign trade is a medium for the economic dependence of poor countries on rich ones. This trade normally constitutes a very large share of a poor economy's activity each year. It is conducted largely with rich partners, roughly following patterns of comparative advantage. For the poor, these advantages are in specialization for exports of primary commodities, goods whose relative worth has been slipping and whose prices are uncertain from year to year. The structure of tariffs only compounds the poor countries' problems by encouraging their continued reliance on primary exports and, simultaneously, by discouraging efforts to move into the more attractive industrial sectors. With a small domestic economic base, and thus limited demand, poor countries face formidable barriers to successful international competition in processed goods. For as long as they specialize in primary products, poor economies will fail to realize the profitability and diversification of spin-off effects.

This set of considerations leads to the propositions (1) that poor countries are export dependent, (2) that this form of economic vulnerability is self-perpetuating, and (3) that their export dependence is intimately tied to their nonindustrial character. As dependence on foreign investment and foreign aid are outlined in the following pages, some qualifications will be made regarding these three statements. Nevertheless, it should be clear that the "benefits" of trade reaped by poor countries from an international division of labor can alternatively be viewed as the means of bare survival in a harsh international trade system. Owing to their extensive reliance on foreign trade, and to their diminutive size by comparison with the industrial countries, control over their economic character and well-being is considerably relinquished to the dominant forces in their environment.

Investment Dependence

Private investments by nationals of one country in businesses located in another country may leave the second country's economy dependent upon decisions made in the first. Basically, there are two forms of private, long-term capital transfers—portfolio investment and direct private investment. Portfolio investment is a purchase that does not imply ownership (government bonds and foreign securities, for example). As such, and also because only about one-fifth of all U.S. foreign investment through 1975 was portfolio,[22] it will not be of further concern here.

Direct private investment, the purchase of ownership shares of a foreign-based operation, can be a source of dependence when it is widespread in a national economy. Whether asymmetrical dependence does in fact result depends on the character of the host society, the interaction between the enterprise and the world market, and the mode of production in which the investments are made.

Direct investment is now commonly identified with "multinational" investment because the ownership of capital sufficient to purchase major shares of a firm is largely confined to businesses that establish new subsidiaries abroad. In definitional terms, "multinational corporations are those economic enterprises . . . that are headquartered in one country and that pursue business activities in one or more foreign countries" by means of ownership of local facilities.[23]

Over the past three decades private investment has experienced two major changes. The first, a quantitative change, is the accelerated growth of total investment abroad. While figures for all countries are not available, it is instructive to note that, between 1965 and 1975, U.S. private direct investment expanded at an average annual rate of about 17 percent. This brought its total book value to more than $133 billion by 1975.[24] It is not surprising, then, that the postwar growth of multinationals has generated a great deal of public and scholarly attention.

The second change in multinational investment represents a new direction, a qualitative change in operations. Prior to 1945, foreign investors concentrated on ownership of minerals and plantations in poor countries. But in more recent times, they have increasingly exported their capital for investment in manufactures rather than in the extraction or cultivation of primary products. Similarly, this investment has been increasingly channeled to other industrially developed and semideveloped economies rather than to less-developed ones.[25] In sum, multinational investment overseas has grown enormously, and principally in manufacturing subsidiaries in other developed countries.

U.S. private investment has conformed to this international pattern. Or, more accurately, it has helped to shape the international investment pattern, since U.S. firms have accounted for about half of all multinational investment worldwide.[26] Not only has U.S. investment growth been extraordinary, but it has become increasingly concentrated in the manufacturing activities of other developed countries, as shown by the figures in Table 2. U.S. investments

Table 2. *U.S. Direct Investment Abroad, 1929–1975*[a]

	1929	1948	1959	1968	1975
Total ($ billions)	8	11	30	65	133
By region (%):					
Europe	19	14.5	16	30	40[b]
Canada	25	31	33	33	23
Latin America	33	39	35	17	17
Other less-developed	23	15.5	16	20	20
By sector (%):					
Manufacturing	24	33	32	41	42
Oil	15	29	33	29	26
Mining	16	10	10	8	5[c]
Utilities	21	11	9	4	27
Other	24	17	16	18	

a All years except 1975 are adapted from Barratt Brown, *Economics of Imperialism*, pp. 208–209; data are from the U.S. Department of Commerce, *Board of Trade Journal*, January 26, 1968, September 23, 1970, and April 7, 1971. The 1975 values are adapted from *Report of the President (1977)*, p. 164, Table 48.

b Includes $3.3 billion in Japan.

c Includes smelting.

in Europe and Canada accounted for slightly less than half of the American total until the 1950s, thereafter growing quickly to 63 percent by 1975. Meanwhile, Latin American and other less-developed countries hosted more than half of the total investment until the 1960s when they dropped, precipitously, to some 37 percent by 1975.

Of course, more direct support of the qualitative shift to manufacturing subsidiaries comes from the lower portion of the table. Manufacturing subsidiaries have grown from one-fourth to two-fifths of total U.S. investment abroad, reflecting a very large swing among new investments toward the processed goods sectors of host economies. In Latin America, the pattern is the same within the region: in the more industrialized countries—Argentina, Brazil, and Mexico—over two-thirds of total U.S. investment by 1970 is in manufactures, whereas, for 1945, the figure stood at only one-third.[27]

The fear of multinational subsidiaries, to be found particularly in poor host societies, is based on a number of considerations, some of which are particular to the type of corporation or subsidiary, and others that are more broadly attributable to the mere presence of large foreign ownership in a small, weak economy. It is to the bases for these latter concerns that are more generally shared in poor hosts that the discussion will soon turn. But this does not mean that multinational investments are totally pernicious. As Hirschman has observed, foreign investment "shares to a very high degree the ambiguity of most human inventions and institutions: it has considerable potential for both good and evil." [28] Recast in his original dependence framework, investment is analogous to trade in that it can have desirable supply effects and, at the same time, undesirable power effects.

Of course, the effects of foreign investment on a poor host society are matters of continuing and sometimes inflamed controversy, with the dependence theorists clearly on one side. Moreover, the debates will probably endure for as long as the evidence remains as elusive as it is now. For ease of discussion, the following review of dependence on foreign investment is organized around four main themes now commonly in dispute: (1) whether and how such investments constitute transfers of valued things from rich to poor countries; (2) the impact of foreign investment on the host's balance of payments; (3) the local social repercussions of multinational subsidiaries; (4) the developmental implications of investment for host economies.

Foreign investment can result in two types of resource transfers from developed parent countries to less-developed hosts: capital and knowledge (including technology).

Capital transfer may come on the occasion of the initial investment in the local subsidiary's construction and equipment. Subsequent expansion or upgrading of equipment may have similar transfer effects. Reinvestment of the subsidiary's profits into its own or other host enterprises will also increase the total stock of capital circulating in the host economy. The firm's payroll is an additional economic stimulant. Finally, if the multinational subsidiary is a new or upgraded enterprise, it is an added source of capital in the form of tax revenues to the host state. However, as already indicated, the presumed benefits of these capital transfers have been seriously questioned.

Regarding the initial investment, many observers are quick to point out that much of the subsidiary's construction and capital goods installation often depends on purchases made in the parent or other developed economies and not in the less-developed host economy, where industrial equipment ranging from irrigation systems to machine goods is rarely available. To the extent that new subsidiaries are increasingly likely to be manufacturers of processed goods rather than producers of raw materials, the purchase of equipment for such capital-intensive enterprises from developed economies increases correspondingly. This situation undermines the benefits that are theoretically assigned to such transfers, although the host benefits to some degree in any case.

Compounding this pattern of initial subsidiary expenditures in developed countries is the practice by multinationals of financing the expansion and upgrading of subsidiaries with local credit. Many times it is the host's lending institutions that put up much of the capital, even though it may then be spent to acquire machinery from a developed country. Indeed, the local capital is often supplied as a lure to the multinational corporation, but when the bait is taken, one negative effect is to reduce the reservoir of domestic capital subsequently available to local entrepreneurs (and to exert some upward pressure on the interest rate for borrowing from a depleted stock).[29] Thus, expansion and upgrading of subsidiaries may also be undertaken without producing a net capital transfer in the forms of either local purchases or parent-supplied financing. Under such circumstances, capital may actually be transferred to the host economy only later, after the enterprise has been established.

Reinvestment of the subsidiary's profits back into the poor host economy is similarly uncertain. In the first place, reinvestment might be aimed at expanding or upgrading the site itself, which, as just discussed, may divert the capital abroad. But profits may instead be "repatriated" to the parent economy (or other developed countries) to avert host taxes or to pay dividends to stockholders of the parent firm of which the subsidiary is an integral part.

As a tax base, the subsidiary's contribution is again mixed. Insofar as the investment does in fact represent capital *added* to the host economy, it provides revenues that the state otherwise would not collect. Regardless of its capital transfer status, the local enterprise provides additional taxes to the extent that its activities heighten taxable production in the host economy.[30] However, these positive tax benefits may be considerably diluted by generous contract provisions, to which the host state is party, that were used to entice the parent firm to locate its subsidiary there initially. Such tax breaks may materialize as tax "holidays" during which few, if any, taxes are due. Alternately or additionally, the state may guarantee for a longer period a lower effective tax than otherwise prevails in the host economy. The multinationals' sharpest critics are quick to see in such tax breaks the pressures on the host government from indigenous economic elites who stand to gain from the presence of the foreign investors.[31]

On balance, then, there are several ways that foreign investment may entail capital transfers to the host economy and state. There are many who argue that the return of profits to the parent country represents exploitative "decapitalization" of the poor host economy. But this line of reasoning misses the point that there may be numerous transfers to the host irrespective of profits made on investments. That is, as Benjamin Cohen has pointed out, "decapitalization means destruction of economically productive facilities" and certainly no destination or use of *profits* can thereby qualify.[32] It is nevertheless true that direct private investment often entails a substantially smaller infusion of foreign capital than its proponents suggest. Raymond Vernon summarizes: "Simply in terms of long-term capital movements, the activities of U.S.-based enterprises would be counted as only marginally important in the less-developed world. The direct investment flow from the United States to the less-developed areas during the 1960s, for instance, came to less than $1 billion annually. This is a modest sum compared with such yardsticks as annual gross capital formation in the less-developed countries, amounting to about $35 billion in the middle of the decade, or annual international resource flows to these countries of about $12 billion."[33]

The second major category of transfer from rich to poor can broadly be conceived as knowledge. Three sorts of knowledge are commonly associated with the activities of foreign investors. The first is organizational or managerial knowledge. The transfer of organizational knowledge refers to the skills learned by native employees hired by the local subsidiary and put to work in managerial positions from foreman or crew chief on up the organizational ladder. In the past, the relevant skills were usually transferred quite slowly as employees worked their way up in the organization through years of tenure and experience. More recently, this learning process has been more systematic, and local talent has been much more successful in advancing in large numbers to very senior positions in the subsidiary's hierarchy. The acceleration of this transfer is largely attributable to host pressures, and is now spelled out as a provision of the host-investor contract in many industries.

In its second variety, knowledge can be transferred as skills related to the techniques required of the productive labor force of the firm. Whether the techniques involved are welding, machinery maintenance, or the servicing of electronic circuitry, the skills are often of potential use in other enterprises. They represent a considerable benefit to the economy's work force that is most often constituted overwhelmingly of low-skilled workers. Whether the local labor pool can assimilate this knowledge is, however, open to question.

Technological transfers are a third type of knowledge that may be disseminated into the host society. The bases for such transfers are two. First, multinational firms generate much technological innovation through their own research and development efforts. Also, their subsidiary network in many countries brings them into extensive contact with new technologies created by others. Thus, their presence in nonindustrial host economies is a prime opportunity for further transfer, especially if the subsidiary is a capital-intensive manufacturer. The new technology it brings, "in conjunction with managerial innovations, stimulates domestic enterprises to improve and modernize their products and procedures in order to remain competitive."[34] Such optimism is open to criticism, of course. For example, the higher interest on local financing mentioned earlier may effectively preclude such quick and easy responses by domestic competitors.

Finally, these knowledge transfers, and particularly those that apply to the work force, are especially apt to upgrade local labor wherever the subsidiary introduces products or technological processes that are new to the host economy.[35] And, of course, the trends toward accelerating foreign direct investment and toward new investment in manufactures are both signs that such knowledge is now being transferred on a larger scale than in times past, although more in the direction of rich countries than poor ones on both these counts.

BALANCE OF PAYMENTS

A less-developed country is usually in chronic need of capital to finance imports necessary to its efforts at economic development. Direct foreign investments play several roles affecting the foreign exchange supply available to the host country. Most discussions focus on one or both of two types of effects—the flow of profits and fees, and the subsidiary's impact on the host's foreign trade.

As noted in the preceding section, profits are very often repatriated to the parent country once a subsidiary is in operation. Further, much of the new investment in capital goods may actually be purchased in developed countries. Add to this the parent firm's charges for royalties, licenses, and service contracts, and the total flow of currency out of the host country may be very large indeed. When weighed against the inflow of capital to the host economy, the balance is usually a net loss to the host. (Over a long period, the host may ultimately benefit directly from increased tax revenues and indirectly by favorable domestic economic changes that the subsidiary stimulates.)

Another way in which investment affects the balance of payments is in the host's foreign trade picture. For example, the foreign-owned enterprise frequently produces goods that otherwise would be imported into the host economy. The effect of such import substitution favors the host's balance of payments by reducing its overseas expenditures. Moreover, the subsidiary is often a successful exporter, thereby generating additional foreign exchange for the poor economy. By way of illustration, some 35 percent of Latin American exports are by U.S.-owned subsidiaries.[36] Finally, these export earnings are especially characteristic of primary goods producers who are commonly positioned at the headwaters of transnational, vertically integrated industrial streams.[37]

In both these ways, then, foreign investment can benefit the host's balance of payments. However, import-substituting industries are usually not primary goods producers, but instead processing facilities. Thus, a host is not apt to realize both types of balance of payments gains simultaneously from the same investment. Finally, primary goods exports entering a vertical oligopoly severely reduce the host's capability of finding alternative markets to that intended by the investor.

The contrary case can be made that import substitution, and thus the multinational subsidiary as a contributor to that process, ultimately reduces the host's exports and foreign exchange earnings.[38] This negative effect on the payments balance derives from the increase in domestic prices that import substitution stimulates, because that price increase will tend to overvalue the nation's currency in the world market. Once again, however, the sketchy evidence is inconclusive regarding the relative strength of this countervailing force.

What can be concluded from these numerous factors working on the host's balance of payments? First, it appears that the flow of profits and various fees back to the parent economy eventually outweighs the opposing movement of investment capital to the host, although this drawback must be discounted by any tax and developmental gains that may ultimately accrue locally. Second, the net effect of import substitution tends to benefit the host's balance of payments if the subsidiary either introduces new products and processes or strongly stimulates exports. Third, it is suspected by observers like Vernon that import-substitution effects are more important than the capital flows, despite the fact that there is as yet no clear answer regarding the net positive or negative payments effects of these two types of factors.[39] If Vernon is correct, then foreign investment is a net gain to the host economy, if not by import substitution then by stimulating its export sector.

SOCIAL REPERCUSSIONS

The foreign-owned enterprise may also have broader effects upon the host society. These repercussions include a number of intangibles. On the positive side, for example, foreign investment collects and organizes both people and information; in the words of one observer, a subsidiary is a "mobilizer of local resources."[40] This mobilization includes transfers of capital and knowledge discussed above. But it also refers to the economic and organizational spin-offs that a production site creates as a variety of auxiliary enterprises develop to support it. This last effect is an economic stimulant to the less-developed society. Further, locally owned auxiliaries create additional vested interests within the domestic business community, interests that must strongly favor preferential treatment toward the foreign investor.

Not surprisingly, these and other repercussions have their darker sides as well. Consider the economic spin-offs themselves. Although the recent trend in new investments favors processed goods, a less-developed economy that continues to host predominantly primary goods producers will develop fewer auxiliary goods and services industries; primary goods tend to be exported from nonindustrial countries in a largely unrefined state, to be processed downstream in an industrial country instead.[41] Where the poor economy hosts a manufacturing subsidiary, more spin-offs are created only at the price of foreign domination in the most sophisticated and profitable—thus the most growth-oriented—sectors of its economy.[42] Additionally, the host government may reorient its economy to support these growth sectors with attendant "distortion" of its own uneven development.[43] Finally, foreign domination in its industrial sectors is heightened by the propensity of the multinational to outcompete local enterprises by virtue of the foreigners' superior technological and organizational skills as well as by their quicker integration into the established world market.[44]

There are other ill effects that can come of the subsidiary's presence.[45] Among these are additional local "distortions," such as the creation, by advertising, of demand for "frivolous" consumer goods. Should the expenditure of scarce national income on Coca-Cola be encouraged in an uneducated, undernourished society? Indeed, this sort of complaint is but one aspect of the more general criticism that the multinational's presence threatens to undermine the host society's cultural identity.[46] Additionally, it is commonly asserted that the multinational firm introduces a productive mode "inappropriate" to its local context. By inappropriate it is meant that the imported technology employs too much capital and too little labor relative to their local supply, hence disproportionate to their relative cost. One consequence of this overcapitalization is that too much of the local payroll will be paid out to managerial employees, as opposed to productive labor, thereby aggravating the host's already-troublesome maldistribution of income. By the same token, however, the restricted number of employees dependent on the foreign presence means that fewer of the total work force will face unemployment should the subsidiary be closed down or relocated in a different host country. Another consequence of capital-intensive subsidiaries is to leave the host technologically dependent, stunting the growth of indigenous research and development spin-off independent of the foreign-owned operation, either by preempting the need for native research scientists and engineers or by hiring them on at the subsidiary.[47]

In sum, these several negative social repercussions stemming from the activities of foreign investors contribute to the broader impression that investment decisions made in the industrial centers of the world are insensitive to the host country's needs, seeking instead only to maximize profit and certainty.[48] Perhaps the most serious consequence of the corporation's pursuit of these goals is, from a host's viewpoint, the possibility that the local subsidiary will be abandoned or moved to another country; subsidiaries have indeed been relocated.[49] However, even if the likelihood is very remote that the subsidiary will shut down—for example, in certain types of mineral extraction where there are very few major concentrations worldwide —the insensitivity of the multinational firm may be evidenced by the subsidiary's failure to understand or conform to the host's plans for national development. Finally, the local frictions and social cleavages engendered by the foreign presence are sometimes reinforced by its simultaneous alliance with local economic elites whose political support for the subsidiary is motivated by the wealth, privilege, and status that they owe to their friendly association with the outsider.

DEVELOPMENTAL IMPLICATIONS

The discussion of a host's costs and benefits has, to this point, presented a largely static conception of investment dependence. It remains now to consider these effects in terms of their impact upon the character of a poor host society and, in particular, the developmental changes in its economic system that may result. An important motive for recruiting foreign investors, after all, is the host's hope that various attendant supply effects will promote its own development ambitions and that, if realized, such growth will allow it to escape its dependence on foreign supplies. This means that a host may hope to maximize short-run supply gains in order to achieve longer-term development objectives.

Economic development, while difficult to define with precision, can be defined to include diverse commodity production, mobility of resources, interconnectedness of different production sectors, and a capacity to generate savings for further investment, all interrelated activities. Thus, economic development can be facilitated by foreign investment transfers that add to the available stocks of capital, knowledge, and technology. A favorable balance of payments helps, too, in that capital resources need not be diverted from domestic application. In other words, greater short-run gains are generally associated with greater long-run gains, and development aspirations further propel sensitivity dependence as a necessary means to a happier end.

It was this logic that prompted nonindustrial countries to invite foreign investment into their economies throughout much of the 1950s and 1960s. More specifically, it was hoped that certain types of foreign investment would serve three valued purposes. First and second, import-substituting plants were sought in pursuit of the dual objectives of maximizing transfers and easing balance of payments problems.[50] Third, because they would produce goods that previously could only be imported, the new firms would reduce the host's need to devote its own resources so extensively to its export industries, themselves typically in less-beneficial primary goods production. This last implication of import-substitution policy would thereby reduce the host's trade dependence.

However, until the "backward linkage" spin-offs and other stimulants to development take hold, the interim is a period of heightened dependence. And even in the longer run there remains the prospect of extensive foreign ownership in the fastest-growing sectors of the host economy. In response to this concern, and to augment the short-run gains accruing to their economies, host governments have increasingly demanded contracts that include timetables for phasing in national ownership and management of foreign operations.[51]

Of course, this is a simplified sketch of the ways in which foreign investment may be tailored to serve as an engine of economic development. A brief reconsideration of some points raised earlier underscores the major dilemma that lies just below its surface. Recall that import substitution entails the production of processed goods. Such production has a relatively high spin-off potential and is likely to feature continuing technological change transferred into the local site by foreign owners. The commodity produced by the firm is probably highly differentiated from its competitors, and the goods may also be destined to enter a vertically integrated world market. Finally, contract provisions may ensure that nationals are rapidly advanced to high positions in management. Since the host actively encourages import-substituting investment in the first place, it is thereby inviting foreign penetration that happens—even if accidentally—to maximize vulnerability dependence by reason of each of the mechanisms just enumerated.

Now, if a policy of import substitution in conjunction with various other measures does in fact work to achieve self-sustaining economic development, that long-term success may well be worth the costs of foreign domination incurred in the intervening years. But recent history amply documents the conclusion that economic development is a tortuous path that many countries have not been able to navigate as yet. In their efforts they have commonly adopted a risky economic strategy that may bear short-run political costs, to discover only later that they are not reaching their development goals and have meanwhile exacerbated their dependence on foreign investment.

PSYCHOLOGICAL EFFECTS

This summary view of the subsidiary's impact on the local economy and society indicates that, for good reason, at least some of the host nationals and leadership feel that their country's fate is substantially dependent upon decisions made abroad and from a very different perspective. Like foreign trade dependence, a heavy reliance on foreign investment represents an economic need that can be immediately met only by persons of another country. Similarly, these two sorts of economic dependence represent a surrender of national sovereignty, or decision-making authority, to foreign elites. But there is a clear difference between dependence on trade and dependence on investment, perhaps a critical one. Although foreign trade and investment both have effects that can be considered in terms of transfers, balance of payments, social repercussions, and developmental implications, investment dependence entails a *foreign physical presence* in the host country. The physical presence of a foreign investor may have a psychological impact so great that it is qualitatively different from the foreign trade counterpart. Accordingly, these *subjective* costs of investment dependence deserve elaboration.

The economic and social effects of a less-developed host's dependence on foreign investment are indeed a mixture of benefits and costs. In contrast, the psychological effects are exclusively negative, and they may have the greater political implications. Distortion in the host country's consumer demands has already been noted. In addition, Blake and Walters hypothesize that multinational corporations act as a lightning rod, drawing a disproportionate share of attention and criticism for their contribution to economic dependence that should, in truth, be attributed to aid and trade ties as well.[52]

Further, there is a consensus that primary goods subsidiaries are much more often the target of resentment than are their industrial counterparts. Several reasons are offered. First, primary goods subsidiaries are thought to be especially offensive because they are so visible. Often located in "enclaves" predetermined by the physical location of the mineral deposits they extract, such industries stand out starkly in otherwise unpopulated locales. Industrial subsidiaries are, on the other hand, located less visibly in urban centers where needed infrastructure (such as transportation and power) and labor are readily available.

Moreover, primary goods production is essentially a static process, changing in character no more than marginally over a long period. Manufacturers, in contrast, may adopt or develop new processes and different products with the passage of time. These more sophisticated enterprises deflect or offset resentment by continuing to offer the local society some transfers of capital, technology, and work skills that primary goods producers eventually exhaust.[53] Extractive enterprises also deplete natural resources. A mining or petroleum operation is therefore an ideal symbol for those who perceive the multinational subsidiary to be sapping the host economy of its potential for betterment.[54] Finally, unprocessed goods are commonly shipped to industrial countries for processing, fabrication, and eventual retail marketing. Host societies may thus come to view their exports as a form of "captive production" in an integrated international system controlled by oligopolies that force low returns on primary goods suppliers, depriving them of any control over the price of "their" commodities.[55]

SUMMARY

The operations of foreign-owned enterprises in less-developed economies have many effects, both good and ill, on the host societies. The extent to which these investments benefit the poor host society in terms of capital and knowledge transfers, accumulation of foreign exchange by favorable impact on its balance of payments position, and numerous social repercussions of the foreign presence is clearly unresolved. The confidentiality that prevents public access to corporate financial records merely heightens the initial impression that these questions of economic and social effects are almost intractably difficult to answer. However, two summary statements can be offered that are germane to the more general concern of investment dependence.

First, private direct investment is a concentration of foreign holdings in the hands of a small number of corporate giants, that is, multinationals. Recall that some four-fifths of U.S. private overseas investment is direct rather than portfolio and that American investments come to half the world total. Now, add to that the fact that in 1969 less than 1 percent of all U.S. firms accounted for 90 percent of all U.S. investment income abroad.[56] The emergent picture is one of great concentration of ownership and control.

The size, growth, and concentrated ownership of foreign investment give substantive meaning to the psychological impact these firms have in less-developed host countries.[57] Indeed, the emotional responses provoked by foreign-owned firms probably owe less to their debatable economic impact than to their mere physical presence. The effects of investment vulnerability on host politics probably owe more to the *appearance* of foreign control in the local economy than to the net of their costs and benefits somehow weighed more objectively.

Aid Dependence

Unlike foreign trade and investment, international aid is a transaction that occurs exclusively between rich and poor. By convention, foreign aid refers to outright grants and to loans made available on concessional terms.[58] These grants and loans are made by individual countries and by multilateral lending agencies such as the International Bank for Reconstruction and Development (World Bank). In addition, foreign exchange is loaned by the International Monetary Fund (IMF) to cover balance of payments deficits. As shall soon become clear, it is useful to include the IMF among foreign aid donors.

Multilateral agencies have assumed an increasingly prominent role as an alternative to bilateral aid sources, accounting for more than one-fourth of the world aid total by the mid-1970s.[59] Multilateral lenders tend to promote general "reform" in the recipient's economic policy as a condition of aid receipt, while individual donors often "tie" their aid by requiring that at least some of it be used by the recipient to buy goods and services from the donor.[60] However, as discussed later, the distinctions between types of donors and conditions of aid agreements are not actually so clear-cut.

Another general trend in recent history has been the decline of foreign aid relative to both private investment flows and export receipts of the less-developed countries. Moreover, despite an absolute increase, foreign assistance declined as a share of donors' national products between 1962 and 1975, as Table 3 shows.

The United States has been giving large scale foreign aid to less-developed countries since 1950. Its assistance has been largely patterned by its cold war "national security" interests, despite official claims that the principal U.S. motive is to facilitate recipients' economic development efforts. Pincus summarizes the official position in the following syllogism:[61] (1) the economic development of less-developed countries is necessary to counter communism and to help build a world of peaceful, independent states; (2) these results favor U.S. interests; (3) economic aid is a catalyst for economic development; (4) therefore, the U.S. should give economic aid to less-developed countries.

Table 3. *Volume of DAC Aid*

	1962	1967	1972	1975
$ Millions (U.S.)	5,438	6,536	8,654	13,585
% Donors' GNP	.52	.42	.34	.43

Note: All years except 1975 are adapted from Organization for Economic Cooperation and Development, *Development Cooperation, 1973 Review* (Paris, 1973), pp. 181, 189. The 1975 aid value is from *Report of the President (1977)*, p. 171, Table 59. The 1975 GNP values are from U.N., *Statistical Yearbook* (1976).

The Development Assistance Committee (DAC) is a subsidiary organ of the Organization for Economic Cooperation and Development. DAC membership is comprised of Australia, Austria, Belgium, Canada, Denmark, France, Germany, Italy, Japan, the Netherlands, Norway, Portugal, Sweden, Switzerland, the United States, and the United Kingdom. DAC aid is official development assistance rather than all aid flows.

As this line of reasoning indicates, economic development and anticommunist motives have been made complementary. In practice the cold war motive has dominated allocation decisions; most U.S. economic aid has been distributed to countries that border communist-governed states, including recipients such as Turkey, Iran, Pakistan, India, South Korea, and South Vietnam.[62]

Excepting the Marshall Plan aid for European postwar recovery, annual U.S. aid reached its apex in the mid-1960s at about $4 billion, declined thereafter to some $3 billion in the early 1970s, and returned to $4 billion in inflated dollars only by the mid-1970s. Measured as a share of its GNP, the allocations dropped more dramatically. U.S. economic aid in 1962, for example, came to 0.56 percent of the GNP, whereas by 1970 the value was down to 0.29, where it remained in 1975.[63] The world decline reported above in Table 3 is thus largely attributable to the United States. But despite general Western and U.S. declines in foreign aid support, a strong case can still be made that foreign aid ties are a source of dependence for the poor recipients. For ease of discussion, the dependence argument is centered around four interrelated factors affected by foreign aid relations—balance of payments, economic development, foreign trade, and foreign investment.

BALANCE OF PAYMENTS EFFECTS

Foreign aid, whether in loans or grants, ordinarily serves one immediate purpose. That purpose is to supply recipients with an ability to pay for imports that they cannot afford solely on the basis of export earnings and capital transfers by direct foreign investment. That is, recipient countries experience a "foreign exchange gap" that aid is intended to fill. The concessionary terms of foreign aid loans, then, are supposed to help pay for imports needed for general economic development. In turn, that development should permit recipients a larger earning capacity in subsequent years when aid repayments fall due. In balance of payments terms, foreign aid is a credit in the year of its receipt, and in years thereafter its repayments are debits.

Donors thereby obviously have direct control over something of value to recipients. Donor countries can withhold or make available bilateral aid with great discretion. Now, the most prominent condition attached to bilateral assistance is that much of it is tied; it must be used to pay for imports from the donor country. In this connection, it should first be pointed out that the face value of tied aid is an inflated estimate of its worth to the extent that the goods and services that a recipient must buy from a donor cost more than prevailing world market prices. Estimates put this overpricing at 20 percent or greater.[64] Second, the United States as the largest bilateral aid source has tied its aid increasingly over time, amounting to more than 90 percent of its annual economic assistance in the last decade.[65] Thus, foreign aid promotes the exports of donor countries by creating captive demand from recipients as a condition of the loans. The overpricing, while reducing somewhat the value of foreign aid to the recipient, has the obvious effect of increasing that country's sensitivity to the donor as a supplier of its imports. Especially as those imports are differentiated, processed goods, the effect of tied aid is to promote bilateralism in trade relations.[66] This last result, as a contributor to vulnerability, probably far outweighs the exaggerated face value of tied aid that must be deflated to estimate its combined dependence effects.

Moreover, even multilateral aid from an international organization is not immune to the wishes of the large industrial countries that pledge to the multilateral body the preponderant shares of its lending power. Indeed, their harshest critics charge that multilateral aid agencies are even more pernicious agents of international economic dependence than their bilateral counterparts.[67] This charge is based on two main premises. First, the few countries that provide most of their operating capital to multilateral lenders such as the IMF and World Bank have great influence over these international agencies' lending decisions. Their influence is due to the weighted voting arrangements that allot member countries voting strength in rough proportion to their respective pledges of capital to the pool that borrowers draw upon. As a prime example of great strength, the "important question" of IMF quota adjustment requires an 80 percent majority vote, leaving the United States in the unique position of being the only member with a formal veto.[68] This formal strength is augmented by the fact that the senior officials of these international bodies are in fact nationals of the very industrial countries that possess such great voting strength. Thus, for example, a U.S. citizen has served as president of the World Bank ever since its creation three decades ago.

The critics' second charge, however, gets more to the heart of the attack on these multilateral institutions. This view has it that efforts by these agencies to encourage "reform" or "monetary stabilization" in recipient economies

actually renders them more dependent than would otherwise be the case, both in terms of sensitivity and vulnerability. Various combinations of several conditions are
tailored to the particular circumstances of specific recipients, but the net result is said to be detrimental to the
balance of payments position of each.

The conditions of aid imposed by these multilateral
agencies, the IMF in particular, are insisted upon only as
the borrower exhausts its first lines of credit. Membership
in the IMF entitles a country to borrow to some extent
with no questions asked, in keeping with the organization's
original intent to provide short-term balance of payments
assistance. However, because poor countries commonly
suffer perennial foreign exchange shortages, they may
quickly come to deplete their unconditional credit, termed
by the IMF the first and second *tranches* (levels). Their
inability to repay principal, plus their continued shortages
of foreign exchange lead the less-developed to dip into the
third *tranche*, where the IMF is authorized to induce
borrowers to pursue economic "reform" programs simultaneously with receipt of further loans. To borrow in the
third *tranche*, an "arrangement with the IMF is negoti-
ated by the affected country's top financial officials (usually the Minister of Finance and the Governor of the Central
Bank) and a team of IMF staff members visiting that country. These negotiations are often hard-fought and bitter." [69]

Of what do these "reform" or "stabilization" arrangements consist? Despite their variations, these loan conditions tend to include the following requirements: (1) abolition or liberalization of foreign exchange and import controls; (2) devaluation of the exchange rate; (3) domestic
anti-inflationary programs (including control of bank credit with higher interest rates and perhaps higher reserve
requirements; control of the government deficit through
curbs on spending, increases in taxes and in prices charged
by public enterprises, and abolition of consumer subsidies;
control of wage rises, so far as within the government's

power; dismantling of price controls); (4) greater hospitality to foreign investment.[70]

What effects might such measures have upon foreign aid dependence?[71] The first, liberalization of foreign exchange and import controls, is an agreement that the aid recipient will (1) liberalize its nationals' ability to exchange domestic currency for foreign currency in order to import commodities of their choice; (2) eliminate prohibitions against the import of certain classes of commodities (regarded as nonessential to development, i.e., "luxury" consumer goods); and (3) curtail multiple exchange rates or variable import duties, each of which was probably structured so as to reduce imports of "nonessential" goods and services. Such new policies would mean, of course, that foreign exchange earnings are less carefully husbanded. In sarcastic understatement, Payer notes that this is "a curious requirement to impose on a country already suffering from a shortage of foreign exchange."[72]

Each of the other three types of requirements—devaluation of the exchange rate, anti-inflationary programs, and greater hospitality to foreign investment—is intended to help counteract the foreign exchange losses incurred by the liberalization of foreign exchange and import controls that heads the list. That is, each of the other three should stimulate the flow of foreign exchange entering the poor economy. But two further effects must be mentioned here.

One byproduct of this typical package of loan conditions is an increase in the openness of the poor economy to penetration by foreigners. Such a program will raise foreign trade both because of the change in exchange rates and because of the liberalization (or even abolition) of exchange and import controls. Additionally, the less-developed economy will be a more attractive site for foreign investors owing to new tax incentives, host provisions of supportive infrastructure (roads, power, and the like), and the attraction of low inflation rates.[73]

The sum of these numerous circumstances is unattractive from the poor country's perspective. For not only is it immediately dependent on foreign aid, it may be forced open to further trade and investment penetration that themselves may become particularly difficult to do without or for which to find alternative suppliers thereafter. Meanwhile, it will experience a continuing foreign exchange gap and mounting debt service obligations.

Servicing their accumulated foreign aid debts by repayment of principal and interest has become a major concern of recipients. Indeed, it has pushed them into portfolio borrowing in the private money markets of commercial banks. The annual repayments of external (public and private) debt by poor countries have been growing about twice as fast as the export earnings they must use to service that debt.[74] As a result, these poor recipients will have to continue to borrow in ever-larger amounts if they intend to maintain (or increase) their annual holdings of foreign exchange with which to buy imports of capital goods and technology for economic development. As Ghana's finance minister put it on the occasion of his reluctant agreement to yet another IMF loan, "the agreement we are signing . . . threatens to sanctify, with the concurrence of our government, the principle of *relieving* debts by *increasing* them."[75]

Nevertheless, foreign aid is so important to poor countries' economic development, as well as to servicing past loans, that they continue to borrow heavily from multilateral and bilateral sources. One estimate has it that all foreign aid taken together accounted for as much as one-third of less-developed countries' gross capital formation in 1964.[76]

ECONOMIC DEVELOPMENT EFFECTS

Investment capital formation is, of course, very close to the heart of less-developed countries' economic development efforts. But the fact that their external debts often grow faster than their ability to repay indicates that recipients' plans for economic development are not necessarily very successfully implemented. Why is this? The answer is by no means simple, but part of the truth may lie in the very act of agreeing to accept foreign aid. More correctly, the *conditions* donors attach to foreign aid may thwart the achievement of developmental objectives that aid is intended to facilitate.[77] And, as indicated earlier, bilateral and multilateral aid agreements include somewhat different conditions to the loans, although both work to stimulate trade and investment dependence as well as further aid dependence itself.

An additional aspect of these external economic relations pertains to the more specific domestic effects that can be expected to result. The general picture may be one of economic deterioration. At the level of the bulk of the population, consumer goods prices may rise, government services may decline, wage hikes may be suppressed, unemployment may expand, and taxes may increase.[78] At a second level, local entrepreneurs will experience higher prices on capital goods, constrictions in available loan capital, higher interest rates on the capital still in circulation, and increased foreign competition in the domestic market.

The sum of these numerous circumstances, should they in fact unfold, is unattractive from the poor country's perspective. Its own development plans would be thwarted as it lost sovereignty over its economic policies. Meanwhile, its vulnerability dependence on foreign trade, foreign investment, and foreign aid would be exacerbated. Thus, its circumstances can be described as a vicious circle, even a downward spiral: a weak economy produces reliance on foreign economic ties that, in turn, depress its economic development and perpetuate its external dependence.

However, this portrayal is incomplete. Heavy emphasis has just been given to the impact of the IMF as an agent of the economic dependence syndrome. It remains to justify why so much weight should be attributed to an agency that, after all, lends only a small minority share of the economic assistance forthcoming from multilateral and bilateral aid programs in the (capitalist) world economy. The *dependencia* explanation lies in the leadership role so often given to the IMF in determining the creditworthiness of prospective aid recipients.

The World Bank and the U.S. Agency for International Development (AID), for example, are mostly concerned with microeconomic aspects of particular projects. The IMF, on the other hand, focuses on macroeconomic conditions whenever members repeatedly fall short of foreign exchange. This broader perspective assumed by the IMF is consistent with the claim that "in some countries the World Bank and the AID rely on the IMF for an assessment of the government's performance, and merely add their weight to that of the IMF by making their support conditional on the country concerned reaching agreement with the IMF."[79]

One illustration of deference among other lenders to IMF judgment was officially acknowledged in the late 1950s. At that time, the Eisenhower administration was advocating an increase in the IMF quota. It was in this context that then-Deputy Secretary of State for Economic Affairs, Douglas Dillon, made the following remarks in testimony before a committee of the House of Representatives: "As an international organization [the IMF] is better able to advise sovereign governments on sensitive matters of financial policy, or to insist on appropriate corrective measures in return for credits, than are other sovereign governments. This, I think, deserves to be underlined. In the delicate area of fiscal and monetary policy, governments find it much easier to accept the counsel of an objective, impartial, and highly competent international organization than the advice of other governments, no matter how good or well-intentioned."[80] One critic of the

IMF summarized its preeminent position among lenders when she wrote:

> The IMF must be seen as the keystone of a total system. Its power is made possible not only by the enormous resources which it controls . . . but more significantly as a result of its function as an international credit agency. All of the major sources of credit in the developed capitalist world, whether private lenders, governments, or multilateral institutions such as the World Bank group will refuse to lend to a country which persists in defying IMF "advice." The real importance of the IMF lies in the authority delegated to it by the governments and capital markets of the entire capitalist world.[81]

Now, whether or not the IMF is in fact the "keystone" of aid dependence, it is true that foreign aid is at least unique in being a "public sector" transaction. In dependence terminology, aid relations are directly within the province of the recipient governments. This difference suggests that aid is a particularly effective vehicle for political influence by the rich country because it can compromise those very elites in the recipient country whose decisions and behavior directly affect the probability of obtaining continued assistance (as well as the amounts obtained). In the words of one observer, public sector assistance "increases the likelihood that the governments of Third World countries will *tolerate* the continuation of massive outflows of private profits and interest on past debts."[82] Indeed, it is plausible to conclude that government officials in recipient countries "have conflicting interests, and are often divided among themselves about the desirability of accepting the conditions attached to IMF loans. . . . However, the key attraction of the funds to which the IMF is the key will usually be decisive, since the method of dispensing aid supports the government budget and relieves it of the necessity of raising new taxes. This conflict of interest explains why government officials will negotiate fiercely about the terms of a [foreign exchange] arrangement but will very rarely break off negotiations in earnest."[83] In other words, these leaders are not only vulnerable to being compromised by their official duties; they are thrust into a conflict of interest because foreign aid strengthens their domestic political base, at least in the short run.

Finally, it should at least be apparent that both bilateral and multilateral foreign aid programs are accompanied by terms that are not clearly of benefit to the economic development of their recipients. In addition to the reasons just reviewed are the effects of foreign aid agreements on both recipients' trade and investment ties to their industrialized partners in the international economic system. Because trade and investment, along with aid, are also specified as mechanisms of dependence, it is worth concentrating briefly on those aspects of foreign aid that are most directly associated with these two other forms of economic ties.

TRADE AND INVESTMENT EFFECTS

Tied foreign aid creates a demand for donor exports, as discussed earlier. In fact, it sometimes permits manufacturers in the donor's economy to export goods that would otherwise find no foreign market because of uncompetitively high prices. The United States, for example, goes a step further by requiring that at least some share of those goods purchased from it be transported in U.S. ships.[84]

More consequential in terms of recipients' trade dependence, however, is that "the most important motive for tying is often the donor's desire to penetrate the recipient's market, in order to create long-run trade ties."[85] Whereas the immediate penalties of tied aid may be calculable by some discounting of the economic worth of the assistance, the further penetration of a recipient by its reliance on increased foreign trade with the donor is likely to have profound effects on the extent and character of economic growth in the poor economy. As discussed in a previous section, liberalization of foreign exchange and import controls brings about that long-run penetration in the recipient's import pattern, with general effects that reduce its ability to husband foreign exchange for purchase of differentiated goods thought essential to its economic development.

As to the recipient's exports, devaluation of the local currency weakens its ability to generate foreign exchange from the sale of its exports in the first place. That is, because its goods are then worth less in foreign currencies, it will accumulate less from its overseas sales.[86] To compensate for this shortage, the poor country is thereby encouraged to devote even more resources to the production of yet greater quantities of those goods for which it has most comparative advantage. Those goods, of course, tend to be primary commodities that provide few spin-offs, perhaps suffer declining terms of trade, and often experience serious price fluctuations. In several respects, then, foreign aid programs can stimulate the recipient's reliance on imports and exports and, at the same time, contribute to the likelihood that the nature of its trade will serve to perpetuate its low level of economic development.

Stabilization measures likewise may encourage foreign investment in an economy already aid dependent. Tax breaks and a low inflation rate are lures to the investor. Infrastructure provisions, resource surveys, and feasibility studies are themselves sometimes financed with foreign aid.[87] Import liberalization promises availability of necessary materials and parts.[88] But, in addition, stabilization programs make foreign takeovers of locally owned enterprises more likely.[89] The sales of domestic firms are slowed by higher-price/suppressed wage recession. Bank credit restrictions make it more difficult than before to borrow needed capital.[90] Thus, the new inflow of foreign capital that is used to buy out local entrepreneurs should be viewed as a resource transfer of discounted long-term benefit to the aid recipient.

Recall, too, that continued receipt of foreign aid also depends on "adequate compensation" to foreign investors for any of their holdings that may be nationalized. For aid dispensed by the United States, this condition was for years specified by the Hickenlooper Amendment.[91] The World Bank and IMF observe the same requirement regarding a recipient's need to "take appropriate steps" to achieve prompt settlement of compensation to private parties.[92] In sum, foreign aid programs encourage potential investors to invest in recipient economies, create conditions that facilitate foreign takeovers of locally owned production facilities, and try to protect foreign investors thereafter.

Finally, it bears repeating that trade and investment dependence are themselves interrelated. On the one hand, foreign-owned enterprises are often among the poor host's major exporting firms, thereby constituting an important source of foreign exchange. Yet foreign investments (usually of another sort) often relieve the host's need for foreign exchange in the first place by producing goods locally that would otherwise be imported. Thus, insofar as the receipt of foreign aid implies repayment burdens, further penetration into the local economy by foreign traders and investors, and stunted economic development, some countervailing consequences are also at work in the forms of export stimuli and import substitution.

Despite these mitigating forces, there is on balance a clear impression that less-developed countries suffer from a continued reliance on foreign aid. Furthermore, stipulations laid down by donors open the recipient to further dependence on foreign trade and foreign investment as well. As one critic observes, "Nations, like individuals, cannot spend more than they earn without falling into debt, and a heavy debt burden bars the way to autonomous action. This is particularly true when one's creditors are also one's customers, suppliers, and employers."[93]

Conclusion

This review of the factors of external economic dependence began with the assertion that the literature lacks orderliness. The ensuing pages attempted to specify and interrelate the contributions of various forms of trade, investment, and aid to the general sensitivity and vulnerability of many poor countries that is denoted by dependence. The following outline of the principal themes covered here is an expansion of Hirschman's scheme concerning trade, with the addition of a third main section for economic development.

A. Policies designed to make it more difficult for partners to dispense entirely with economic relations.
   1. Increase the partners' gains from relations.
      a. With respect to trade:
         (1) develop exports in articles enjoying a monopolistic position in other countries and direct trade to such countries.
         (2) direct trade toward poorer countries.
         (3) improve the partners' terms of trade.
      b. With respect to investment:
         (1) invest in production that continues to exhibit technological change.
         (2) invest in production that is import substituting.
         (3) invest in production that has low visibility.
      c. With respect to aid, do not tie aid to the recipients' imports.
   2. Increase the partners' adjustment difficulties in case of severance of relations.

    a. With respect to trade:
- (1) trade with countries with little mobility of resources.
- (2) induce in the partners' economies a wide discrepancy between the pattern of production for exports and the pattern of production for home consumption.

    b. With respect to investment:
- (1) invest in poor countries.
- (2) invest in labor-intensive production.
- (3) invest in production for export into vertically integrated industries.
- (4) condition foreign aid on compensation for nationalized investments.

    c. With respect to aid:
- (1) give aid to poor countries.
- (2) encourage a foreign trade deficit.
- (3) encourage large debt service burdens.

3. Create vested interests in the partners' societies and tie the interests of existing powerful groups to the economic relations.

    a. With respect to trade, direct trade toward poor countries.

    b. With respect to investment:
- (1) invest in production with large infrastructure needs.
- (2) invest in production with high spin-off volume.
- (3) advance nationals to leadership positions in firms.

    c. With respect to aid, give aid to governments having precarious bases of domestic support.

B. Policies designed to make it difficult for the partner to *shift* to alternative suppliers:

   1. With respect to trade:

    a. Direct trade toward smaller countries.

      b. With respect to the exports of the trading partners:
- (1) import products for which there is little demand in other countries.
- (2) drive prices of the export products of the trading partners above world prices.

      c. With respect to the imports of the trading partners, export highly differentiated goods creating consumption and production habits.

  2. With respect to investment:
- a. Invest in smaller countries.
- b. Invest in highly differentiated import-substitution manufacturing creating consumption and production habits.
- c. Invest in enterprises for exports into vertically integrated production.

  3. With respect to aid:
- a. Encourage large debt service burdens.
- b. Tie aid to imports.

C. Policies designed to prevent partners' economic development.

  1. With respect to trade, encourage primary goods exports.

  2. With respect to investment:
- a. Invest in primary goods production.
- b. Invest in export industries to serve a vertically integrated market.

  3. With respect to aid, condition bilateral aid on IMF loan approval for recipients reaching the third *tranche.*

To develop a set of prescriptions for dependent countries requires only that obverse entries be made in a parallel framework. Some contradictory prescriptions within this outline emerge as one compares the third main section with the first and second. For example, dependence is greater as the partner receives larger benefits from, say, industrial investment that promises continuing technological improvements. Investment in raw materials extraction, however, is preferable if the aim is to retard the host's economic development. Each prescription would, in principle, heighten long-run vulnerability. This and other such contradictions represent the broader conflict between relations that, on the one hand, may increase the partner's gains and hence its sensitivity costs if relations are interrupted and, on the other hand, minimize its gains insofar as they might advance its economic development. In other words, the short-run and long-run goals of either partner are in some ways mutually inconsistent.

Additional inconsistencies arise even within the confines of the first and second sections. One illustration concerns foreign aid dependence. There, one can see the pull between the dependence that rises in direct proportion to the worth of the aid received and the opposite attraction of tying aid to inhibit the recipients' capacities to shift trade suppliers, a tactic that reduces the worth of the aid. The broader implication of all the contradictions implied in this chapter is that international economic dependence is not a simple phenomenon. Instead, it has considerable theoretical complexity. Further, those concerned with dependence must weigh the competing contributions of the several forces involved.

Of course, the conception of international economic dependence presented here still reflects the guiding interests raised initially: dependence entails both sensitivity and vulnerability to foreigners' decisions. In keeping with this conception, the study treats foreign trade, aid, and investment as alternative or complementary modes of penetration into a national economic system. Their effects are additive in that the *form* of outside economic control is thought to be of very little consequence as compared to the *extent* of that control. A dependent economy is one that is open to foreign manipulation, especially if faced with the possibility of high long-term cost. Thus, if foreign trade is a source of dependence for a given country, a further increase in foreign trade will result in proportionally greater dependence. Similarly, an increase in foreign aid will correspondingly inflate the recipient's dependence, and added foreign investment will deepen the dependence of the host country. In short, this conception is distinguished by the proposition that a certain amount of dependence on, say, trade is about equivalent to the same amount of aid or investment dependence; the three sorts of transactions are conceived as having additive impacts.

An implicit restatement of this additivity comes from a quite different perspective. Trade, investment, and aid have been interrelated throughout this chapter. But when they are viewed instead over the broad sweep of history—from nineteenth-century imperialism to contemporary dependence—they can be linked by the thesis that trade penetration has been partially displaced by investment and aid ties.[94] Colonialism entailed the creation of export enclaves to serve the mercantilist objectives of the metropoles. As colonial territories became legally independent, the nature of their economic dependence changed for several related reasons. First, after independence, the former metropoles were no longer able to dictate that the export-oriented imbalance in the weak economies be continued. Many of the new states then quickly began to reorient their economic activity toward greater domestic production and consumption. Closely related to this change has been the adoption by many weak states of a conscious policy of import-substitution industrialization to reduce their trade dependence. But, because their economies provide opportunities for only slow capital accumulation, the new governments have permitted or even encouraged entry of foreign investment and aid to speed the process of local industrialization. Such an evolution has meant that import substitution often entails substitution of another sort as well, namely, the partial displacement of trade dependence by reliance on foreign investment and aid loans. Finally, insofar as the poor country thereby succeeds in building an industrial base, those industries may further open the economy to additional foreign investment by creating spin-off opportunities that outsiders seize. The net result of such an evolution from imperialism to a "new dependence" is a continuation, albeit in different form, of foreign economic control over a still-dependent economy. This scheme of evolutionary substitution constitutes an implicit statement that the means of penetration are less consequential than the sensitivity and vulnerability they produce.

Strictly speaking, all of this does not deny the possibility that foreign aid may be the leading edge of dependence, nurturing a more pervasive, malignant form of the syndrome. For if aid is a catalytic agent to trade and investment dependence, then one would expect them all to be present in a penetrated economy. After all, a parallel case could be made, for example, to the effect that investment in unprocessed goods brings about declining terms of trade and hence a perennial foreign exchange shortage that, in turn, results in foreign aid indebtedness. Either way, the end result is dependence of all three forms.

This study is ultimately concerned with the foreign policy consequences of economic dependence rather than with interrelations among economic sources of political vulnerability. For a country that finds itself economically vulnerable to the decisions of another is often thought to pursue a *political* course characteristically different from countries not vulnerable. The following chapter develops the theoretical bases for expectations about certain political consequences.

Chapter 3
Foreign Policy Compliance

Numerous political issues lurk in the background of the preceding discussion on economic dependence. For example, tariff restrictions to protect domestic producers from foreign trade competitors may be the price a government must pay if it is to have political support at home among those whose livelihood derives from the protected enterprises. Second, donor governments have tried to use foreign aid allocations as a means of securing the overseas investments of its citizens and corporations. Finally, the distribution of U.S. foreign aid itself follows clearly the political principle of supporting most those recipients perceived to be especially susceptible to communist influence. Thus, the links of trade, investment, and aid that bind a dependency to a dominant country may be substantially affected by a host of political considerations.

On the other side of this coin is the prospect that political behavior can be affected by international economic ties. While the above illustrations serve to show how politics can affect economics, the obverse must also be considered. One may well ask how economics affect politics.

The notion of *exchange* is useful here. Economic relations between dominant and dependent countries are modes of exchange. In their bilateral foreign trade each is exchanging commodities and currencies with the other. Similarly, foreign investment is an exchange of capital and skills invested in return for which profits at some later time are anticipated. Foreign aid loans follow the same pattern whereby the lender expects repayment with interest in the future. The second chapter described the asymmetrical economic effects of these economic exchanges. This chapter explores the possibility that, in their foreign policy behavior, dependencies are offering support to the foreign policy objectives of the dominant state. Their support may be grudging, but it may be necessary because the dominant state has asymmetric control, especially in the long-run, over the costs and benefits to be derived from their economic relations. This means that *the foreign policy behavior of dependencies is viewed as partial payment in exchange for the maintenance of benefits they derive from their economic ties to the dominant country*. The inquiry centers on the following question: In their foreign policy behavior, are dependencies compliant with the preferences of their dominant economic partners? Or, put differently, do dependent countries place an equal or lower value on their foreign policy behavior than on their international economic relations? [1]

The discussion to this point has raised two conceptual issues that deserve some elaboration. First, it is not clear at just what point domestic politics leave off and foreign policy begins. Second, an investigation of behavioral compliance requires that compliance be distinguishable from other behavior.

Conceptual Distinctions

It was long presumed that national governments act in two separate arenas, the domestic and foreign. This meant that their policies and actions were targeted toward circumstances internal and external to their geographical boundaries, and that policy actions directed toward one domain seldom affected the other. However, countries' experiences have increasingly challenged this presumption that domestic politics are generally isolated from foreign relations.

A conceptual and empirical attack on such isolation has been galvanized by James Rosenau's attention to "linkage politics."[2] Rosenau's assessment that there are many links between the domestic and foreign policy arenas has historical precedents. But particularly at his urging there has recently emerged a research movement that is self-consciously devoted to a systematic understanding of such linkage phenomena. The linkage metaphor, whether or not it offers any new insights, well reflects the interdependent nature of contemporary international relations.[3] The perspective of political economy adds a second dimension to the matter under study here—behavioral consequences of asymmetrical linkages between international and national economics and politics.

Foreign policy decisions of economic dependencies constitute what Rosenau calls "adaptive behavior."[4] But one may ask, "Adaptive to what?" The answer is: adaptive to pressures exerted by forces both within and without the polity. Foreign policymakers must ultimately make important choices for their societies under the constant goading of both domestic and foreign pressures. These influences on government leaders, forces to which they adapt, are in part attributable to linkages of political economy that exist between foreign and domestic actors.

The nature of the linkages considered in this research warrants further elaboration. The second chapter argued that foreign trade, aid, and investment have direct impact on the domestic economics of dependencies, affecting such things as specialization of production, domestic price levels, availability of local capital and growth of indigenous industry, tariffs, and foreign debt. Such domestic effects, it was asserted, contribute in circular fashion to continued economic dependence on foreigners. At this broad level, what can be said of the politics of these economic linkages?

Because they are elaborated in the next section, the accompanying politics shall only be flagged here. But what emerges, not surprisingly, is that politics and economics are thought to co-occur. That is, for each analytic link among economic forces and activities already discussed, there is also a political component. Among the politics already mentioned are the calculations by dominant countries of the strategic advantages to be had by creating and nurturing economic dependencies. This is a theme that is commonly found, for example, among students of superpower competition for influence in less-developed countries: since U.S. policymakers associate signs of Third World "turbulence" with the threat of communism, they deal with such immediate problems "as part of a global contest for ideological and military supremacy."[5] However, such cold war motivations are somewhat beyond the bounds of immediate interest. Other, more specific politics are of concern here, and they are considered to influence the foreign policy behavior of dependencies. Categorized according to their sources, there are four discernible groupings emanating from (1) the governments (or states) of dominant countries, (2) the states of less-developed countries other than dependencies under scrutiny, (3) economic groups within dependent societies, and (4) the states of dependencies.

Generally speaking, a dominant state has two relevant concerns. On the one hand, it is interested in promoting the stability of governments in its economic sphere. Reasons for this may include such commonplace explanations as its interest as a major power in promoting the status quo, its desire to preserve "friendly" governments within its influence network, its perceived obligation to protect the foreign economic ventures of its own citizens, and its commitment to the promotion of economic development in poor countries. On the other hand, a dominant state also hopes to draw support from other governments for some of its foreign policy objectives. When it believes that concurrence by other countries is of value, its dependencies are among those governments most likely to be approached. For example, one United States senator, "expressing a common resentment," publicly voiced his impatience with foreign aid recipients that failed to support the U.S. in its opposition to China's admission to the United Nations. Said Senator Hugh Scott, "A good many nations we have helped generously with foreign aid over many years have shown a classic lack of appreciation." [6]

A second source of political motivations stems from the influence on dependencies of other less-developed countries. All less-developed countries have their poverty in common. They also share to a considerable extent an inability to reverse their economic circumstances by individual action. Accordingly, they have attempted in several ways to act collectively. The politics of their concerted action are nowhere more visible than in the Organization of Petroleum Exporting Countries (OPEC) and the United Nations Conference on Trade and Development (UNCTAD). OPEC has not only been able to control production and price levels of crude oil available on the world market, it has also achieved for its Middle East members spectacular political payoffs. Less dramatically, UNCTAD has legitimized and formalized the political prominence of economic resource distribution between rich and poor countries. Indeed, it is partly because of UNCTAD that such questions of political economy have come to dominate proceedings of the General Assembly. And, since each delegation to the U.N. has one Assembly vote, dependencies find themselves among the large voting majority on just such issues. In sum, because of global and regional associations such as these, a dependency may be aroused, or even pressured, to take foreign policy stances that it would reject if it were acting in isolation from other poor countries. Alternatively, it may be similarly emboldened by a demonstration effect; simply witnessing the nonconformity of a Castro or Allende may encourage a dependency to act defiantly.

Various domestic groups are also concerned with their government's foreign policy. In the context of economic dependence, groups of particular interest here are indigenous business elites. Some of them are supportive of foreign policies that have the effect of continuing economic dependence because the links of trade, investment, and aid from abroad advance their own businesses. Their support will reinforce foreign policymakers who perceive a need to keep open the international economic lifelines that promote their survival in office. Indeed, these economic elites may themselves hold high office. The dependent state would find the success of many of its promised programs thwarted, even to the point of economic collapse for the society, if it were greatly to offend the dominant state by pursuing what was, to the latter, an "unsatisfactory" course in its foreign policy.

However, countervailing pressure is put on the state by those other elites who instead regard dependence as a depressant or a threat to their economic activities. This latter set of elites, drawing as well on support from discontented sectors of the public, may be a force to be reckoned with. At the least, they may compel their government to exhibit foreign policy behavior that is sometimes resistant to the preferences of the dominant state. More forcefully, their opposition to foreign economic dominance may be channeled toward support for the political opposition whose foreign policy behavior, upon accession, they would presumably countenance. Sunkel describes the Latin American experience this way:

> The consequent mobilization of the new social forces
> that have emerged from the process of industrialization,
> urbanization, state intervention, and increased educa-
> tion . . . has led in some cases to the overthrow of the

traditional dominant classes (sometimes by military regimes), or at least has wrested from them internal reforms and a renegotiation of their international relations. In some countries these traditional dominant
classes have opposed such pressures by increasing coer-
cion and internal repression and by seeking even more
outside support. Nevertheless, in most cases, certain internal reforms have been tried, reforms that almost necessarily imply the adoption of "revisionist" positions
with respect to the United States.[7]

Thus, even though resistant foreign policy behavior may
not lessen the ties of dependence, it may serve a symbolic
purpose that assures the government a better chance of
survival in office.

A final locus of political motivations is the dependent
government's officials themselves. In addition to their in-
stincts for political survival, they may feel duty-bound to
act "in the national interest." However the national interest is operationally defined, foreign policy behavior so motivated may sometimes be inconsistent with the foreign
policy position of the dominant country. And, as suggested
already, the "national interest" may come to be reshaped
by the influence of other poor countries, too.

This brief survey of the kind of politics that accompany
economic dependence should make clear that the character
of a dependency's foreign policy behavior is not necessarily obvious or simple. Elites within the poor country may
be greatly at odds with each other. Moreover, the preferences of the dominant country may differ from those of
the dependent state, and perhaps from other poor countries
from which the latter draws inspiration. However, despite
the presence of numerous political motivations and pressures from several sources, the foreign policy behavior of a
dependent country will be, as it adapts to all of them, more
or less in accord with the preferences of the country that
dominates its economic life. It is this consequence of politi-

cal accord that calls for an understanding of what is meant by behavioral "compliance."

Compliant behavior is deferential.[8] It is behavior that accedes to the wishes of others. This means that its wellsprings are external rather than internal to the actor.[9] The further implication is that, as one actor complies, a second party can be said to have influenced the first successfully. Of course, in principle two actors may behave congruently in the absence of any influence relation, but this is concurrence instead. Thus, over a series of occasions where two actors behave congruently, some portion of their activities may reflect concurrence while the remainder is demonstration of compliance.

Notice that this conception of compliance dovetails with earlier discussions of political economy in the relations between a dominant country and its dependencies. Political compliance becomes an unwritten condition of economic transactions between unequals. Or, to put the matter somewhat differently, a dependency's foreign policy compliance can be considered an integral part of the exchange. This is not to say that a dependency will comply on every occasion on which it does not already concur. The government of a dependent economy is also motivated to resist compliance in pursuit of its own divergent national interests, in response to disgruntled domestic elites and disaffected publics, and in conjunction with other poor countries; it is adaptive to diverse and competing forces. Therefore, once these cross-pressures are acknowledged, propositions characterizing the foreign policy behavior of a dependency must make assumptions regarding the recognition and relative weights of the several factors. However, despite the fact that a large number of combinations of factors is conceivable, further speculation is confined to a relative few. By this reduction, the following discussion can be restricted to four characteristic forms of proposed foreign policy behavior of a dependency, three of them static and the other one dynamic in character.

Four Compliance Propositions

Three of the four propositions developed here are competing statements of the extent to which a dependency's foreign policy behavior will conform to that of the country that dominates its economics. However, even though the first three propositions differ from one another, it bears repeating that all four of them embrace the notion that a country's foreign policy behavior is rank-dependent.[10] For example, in each case it is assumed that the dominant nation consistently exerts asymmetrical economic pressure on the dependency to induce the latter's compliant political behavior. Such pressure may not often, if ever, be made explicit; an occasional mention may well be sufficient to remind the dependent state's decision-makers of their country's economic vulnerability. Indeed, their knowledge of the dominant country's latent economic arsenal may suffice to generate political compliance. Each of the propositions regarding compliance, then, reflects the premise that nations' respective ranks dispose a dominant country to expect or even pursue its dependencies' political compliance by virtue of its superordinate rank. On the other hand, the first three propositions differ according to their respective assumptions regarding the nature of, and the extent to which, additional pressures are felt by the officials of low-ranking, dependent countries. The foreign policy behavior predicted by each is a differing mode of adaptive response.

LINEAR COMPLIANCE

The first of these propositions is the simplest. It begins with the assumption that the foreign policy behavior of a dependency is constrained only by its economic dependence. Accordingly, the expectation is that the greater the extent of a country's dependence, the greater is its political compliance. As illustrated in Figure 1, this proposition posits a

FIGURE 1. *Linear Compliance*

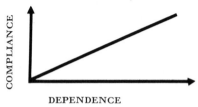

direct, linear relationship between dependence and compliance.[11] There are two ways that this expectation can be justified.

In keeping with the assumption that dependence is of paramount importance in determining a dependency's behavior, it is sometimes argued that the shackling is a direct result of the foreign penetration of its economy sensed by its foreign policymakers. Economic dependence "is founded on the exploitation of economic vulnerabilty and sanctions need not be put into effect or even spelled out explicitly in diplomatic contacts for the desired result to be produced." [12]

Dominance and dependence are, of course, references to a hierarchical ordering of units. In his impressionistic study of international hierarchy, Steven Spiegel takes very much the same tack in saying that the foreign policy choices of low-ranking governments are severely constrained by their dependence on other countries. Dividing countries into seven strata, he begins by asserting that "the acts of the most powerful determine the policies" of many lower-ranking members of the international system. Moreover, only the most powerful countries "are able to influence and even direct the policies of countries of all sizes and strengths." [13] From these hierarchical relations, a dominant country generates for itself various benefits from the weaker governments' public and private behavior. Such behavior, Spiegel notes, is apt to include "the positions of their diplomatic representatives and the direction of their foreign policies." [14]

A second explanation of the proposed direct linear relationship between economic dependence and political compliance is only slightly more complicated than the first. In this case, the argument is made that the economic interests of business elites within the dependency are advanced by the foreign economic penetration that characterizes the country. These elites, then, find it in their private self-interest to act so as to guarantee the continuance of those economic relations. Thus, they exert pressure on their government to behave in ways thought most likely to perpetuate those economic flows, including their state's foreign policy compliance with the preferences of the dominant state. In sum, this explanation requires that these self-interested elites exist, and that they exert such influence on their government.

Johan Galtung is among those who believe that both of these requirements are met in dependent societies. [15] He refers to these domestic elites as the "bridgehead" of dependence. Further, he attributes their collaboration with the dominant country to the "harmony of interest" between elites of different countries, where the concrete nature of those interests is often defined by economic transactions between their rich and poor economies. The identity and motives of those local elites are considered in the following passage (on Latin America), which represents an archetype of marxist commentary:

Clientele classes [in dependencies] are those which have a vested interest in the existing international system. These classes carry out certain functions on behalf of foreign interests; in return they enjoy a privileged and increasingly dominant and hegemonic position within their own societies, based largely on economic, political, or miltary support from abroad. In this sense the clien-

tele classes come to play in Latin America today the
role historically performed by the *comprador* bourgeoisie (export-import mercantile elites, whose strength, interests, and very existence were derived from their function in the world market). Like their behavior, the
ideologies of these classes reflect their dual position as
junior partners of metropolitan interests, yet dominant
elites within their own societies. The clearest example of
clientele classes today are those elements of the Latin
industrial bourgeoisie which "expand and thrive within
the orbit of foreign capital [whether as] wholesalers . . .
or as suppliers of local materials to foreign enterprises
or as caterers to various other needs of foreign firms
and their staffs. . . ."

The state bureaucracy and other sectors of the middle
class—for example, technical, managerial, professional
or intellectual elites—become clientele when their interests, actions, and privileged positions are derived from
their ties to foreign interests. Particularly with the expanded role of the state in the national economy, the
state bureaucracy . . . has been viewed by some as the key
to national autonomy. Nevertheless, when the primary
function of the state is to stimulate private enterprise,
when the private sector is largely controlled by foreign
interests, and when the state bureaucracy itself relies on
material and ideological support from abroad, . . . the
"autonomy" of the state bureaucracy must be illusory.

The alliances and conflicts of clientele classes with
other domestic classes are shaped to a considerable extent by their previous and present alliances with foreign
interests. Thus, for example, no less important than the
alliances or conflict of a Sao Paulo industrialist with the
Brazilian proletariat or coffee-growing interests are his
economic and ideological alignments with Wall Street
bankers or foreign industrial interests; indeed the former are often shaped by the latter. The existence of
these clientele classes in the dependent nation, whose

interests correspond to those of the dominant classes in the dominant nations, is the kingpin and the *sine qua non* of dependency.[16]

Very similarly, nonmarxist Marshall Singer describes the insinuation of "comprador" interests into the circle of government policymakers: "It is simply a reality of life that in almost every country of the world the [government's] decision-making elite tends to be recruited from (or closely related to) the country's major economic interest groups. And if . . . a large share of a country's G.D.P. [Gross Domestic Product] is derived by trade with one particular country, there is a very strong likelihood that the decision-making elite in the dependent country will in some way be bound to that foreign country."[17] Singer adds that if such elites sometimes find their economic and national identities to conflict, "they may well support the former over the latter. More often, however, they will use their influence as members of an indigenous elite to view their personal economic interest as a national interest worthy of government support."[18]

These commentators seem to agree that compliance and dependence covary in linear association, either because the dependent state is fearful of the latent threats posed by foreign economic dominance and/or by virtue of the impact on the foreign policymakers of self-interested business elites who profit from the ties of dependence. Furthermore, both theses regard the dependency's political behavior as responsive to external economic conditions, although the second opens an indirect channel for influencing the adaptive government of the dependency.

Now, it may seem that this first proposition is too simplistic to warrant serious consideration. After all, even with the insertion of a role for collaborative local elites, this portrayal of pressures on the dependent state fails to consider its adaptation to several forces alluded to earlier that are, in fact, countervailing. For example, what about

the resistance of constrained foreign policymakers themselves to obeisant denial of their divergent national interests? It was precisely this criticism of "oversimplification"
that Patrick McGowan and Klaus-Peter Gottwald anticipated in their study of the foreign policy behavior of black
African states: "African foreign policy behavior, while
adaptive, is more influenced by national attributes and
linkage phenomena (Rosenau, 1966, 1969) than the traditional emphasis on personalities and ideologies suggests
(Mazrui, 1967a, 1967b; McKay, 1966). Within a context
of powerlessness and dependence, character and ideas alone
cannot overcome a passive-subordinate role in international affairs."[19] Of course, others *do* disagree with this assessment and, therefore, offer alternative views regarding the
association between dependence and compliance.

DECREASING MARGINAL COMPLIANCE

A second broad proposition that can be distilled differs
from the linear one by virtue of the addition of one or
more types and sources of political pressure felt by dependent governments. That is, although adherents to the
second proposition may admit the relevance of both of the
forces considered already, these observers converge on a
different postulated association between compliance and
dependence by introducing additional ingredients into the
scheme. Once again, all determinants can be at least partially attributed to the fact of economic dependence itself.
The thread that pulls together the contributors to the second proposition is their attention to a dependency's "national interest" that is not fully consistent with the national
interests of the dominant country. (Therefore, they might
well be among those who regard the linear proposition as
simplistic.)

Foreign policymakers in the dependency may sometimes
view their nation's interests as best served by behavior that

is at odds with the wishes of the dominant state. That is, they may view the national interest as encompassing concerns in addition to safeguarding the sustenance provided by their extensive economic ties to the dominant nation. There may be specific issues, such as their disposition toward a third country's politics, on which they are unwilling to compromise extensively their departure from the official stance of the dominant country. The first foreign policy act of the new Allende government was to renew diplomatic relations with Castro, in stark contrast to U.S. efforts to ostracize Cuba from relations with any of its hemispheric neighbors. Similarly, dependencies may resist the dominant state's promulgation of an international economic or security agreement that they regard as detrimental to their own economic or military fortunes. Again, such divergent national interests are illustrated by the foreign policy professed by the Chileans in 1970:

The international policy of the popular government [under Allende] will be directed toward affirming the complete political and economic autonomy of Chile.

There will be diplomatic relations with all countries of the world, irrespective of their ideological and political position, on the basis of respect for self-determination and the interests of the people of Chile. . . .

The position of active defense of Chilean independence implies denouncing the OAS as an instrument and agency of North American imperialism and to struggle against all forms of Pan-Americanism implicit in this organization. The popular government will opt for the creation of an organism that is truly representative of Latin American countries.

It is considered indispensable to revise, denounce, and ignore, according to individual cases, the treaties or agreements that mean compromises, that limit our sovereignty, and concretely the treaties of reciprocal as-

sistance, the mutual assistance pacts, and other pacts
that Chile has signed with the United States.[20]

Notice, too, that this passage suggests a felt need to assert
national sovereignty itself, quite apart from specific issues
and agreements. In Chile, in response to a growing public
and elite movement against economic dependence, government leaders "felt a mandate" to try to achieve Chilean
control "over its own economic and political life" predat-
ing Allende's election by many years.[21]

Thus, whether or not divergent national interests are
issue-specific, their general effect would be to diminish the
extent of aggregate behavioral compliance first proposed.
Graphically, such a reduction takes the form of decreasingly compliant behavior on the part of those dependencies
initially proposed to be most seriously constrained by their
economic vulnerabilities, as illustrated in Figure 2. Decreasing marginal compliance depicts situations in which

FIGURE 2. *Decreasing Marginal Compliance*

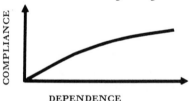

DEPENDENCE

countries whose dependence is relatively low would often
comply with the dominant state, much like the situation
described by the first proposition. However, decision-
makers more seriously constrained by higher levels of economic dependence would further comply to a decreasing
extent because they are also motivated to follow divergent
national interests that cannot be altogether suppressed or
ignored. In principle, then, countries most greatly dependent may even be at the point that their compliance is no
greater than that of dependencies whose economies are

slightly less vulnerable to foreign control; divergent national interests may finally not be amenable to further compromise.

Compliance, as noted, is viewed here as one part of an exchange between dominant and dependent countries. A dependency receives economic utilities from the dominant country and, in turn, provides the latter with foreign policy support. From this perspective derives an alternative justification for the decreasing marginal compliance captured in Figure 2. Although a dependency's compliance is considered to be of value, the dominant state may regard that compliance as having decreasing marginal utility. In other words, the dominant state may think a dependency's accord with its foreign policy positions to be decreasingly important beyond some threshold of international support that it deems minimally satisfactory. If so, then once the accord of others is sufficiently widespread or frequent, further demonstrations of agreement—including those of its economic dependencies—increasingly fail to be cultivated. Furthermore, if this is true, the dominant state would be decreasingly prone to regard economic rewards or sanctions as mechanisms for inducing the other country's support beyond the sufficiency threshold. Thus, the extremely dependent country would not be pressured to comply at a correspondingly higher level than would be another country less vulnerable in economic terms.

In sum, the expectation that compliance declines at the margin accounts for more factors than does the linear compliance prediction advanced first. The additional factors that may lead to decreasing marginal compliance are, quite simply, a blend of different motivations on the part of governmental officials in a dependency, some of their constituents, and perhaps the dominant state. As a result, neither a dominant nor dependent country may perceive that the dependency's complete compliance serves its "national interests," broadly construed.

DEFIANCE

If pressures to comply may encounter competing forces representing some sense of a dependency's divergent national interests, there is another form of resistance that is even more powerful. This is the power of resentment which, if acute, may overcome motives to comply, producing defiant behavior instead. To be sure, a dependency's defiance may invite economic reprisal by the dominant country; defiance, after all, is viewed here as a failure to satisfy the unwritten rules of exchange between the two countries. Nevertheless, the dependent state may chafe enough in the yoke of subordination that it is willing to assume the economic risks that defiant foreign policy behavior would entail.

Where is the locus of such powerful resentment? Its genesis may be the local entrepreneurs' inability to compete with foreign-owned competitors in the dependent economy. Or it may stem from a more widespread sense of injustice in reaction to foreign influence over the country's economic policies. Writing in 1963, Raymond Vernon cautioned:

> Make no mistake about the direction from which these forces come [in Latin America]. Only a tiny part of the pressure to curb the foreigners comes from Marxists. Only a little more comes from the national socialists. Much more probably comes from those who in a fine rage are indiscriminately against all the symbols of the old order—symbols that, as they see it, include the landlords, the generals and the foreign investors.
>
> But finally, importantly, there are the pressures from the new business class, the new technicians, the new administrators. These are the men who feel fully as competent as the foreigner to run their national industries and who are impatient to prove that fact to themselves and the world.[22]

He then predicted that Latin American governments could not "stand up against such forces for very long."

Further, the decision-makers themselves may resent their external dependence on trade, investment, and aid: "The political implications of aid may be ignored by the recipients or assistance may simply backfire for the donor as the recipient regime turns hostile [because] the donor may be resented for its wealth." [23] Finally, a dependency's resentment of foreign dominance may be prompted, or at least augmented, by the outcries and behavior of other poor countries that feel similarly plundered by rich oppressors.

Thus, resentment may emanate from several possible sources. Of more immediate concern is the defiance it may generate in dependencies' foreign policy behavior. And, at this point, the discussion becomes quite speculative, if only because the pattern of behavior springing from affective phenomena such as resentment is difficult to predict in advance. In other words, insofar as resentment leads dependencies to violate the terms of exchange—to defy rather than comply—the occasions and frequency of their defiance are difficult to anticipate because emotions sometimes have their own dynamics.

With this caveat in mind, however, assume that there is a direct correspondence between a dependency's level of resentment and its propensity to exhibit defiant foreign policy behavior: the greater its resentment, the more frequent will be its defiance. Since it has already been argued that dependence can breed resentment, a *logical* conclusion is that the greater the extent of its dependence, the more frequent will be a dependency's defiance.

If this is a defensible argument, it remains incomplete without attention to the countervailing motivations to comply. For ease of presentation, assume that the inclination to comply is in linear association with the extent of dependence, as asserted in the first proposition. Coupled, then, with the opposing tendency to defy in direct linear relation to the extent of dependence, the net result in terms of manifest compliance would follow a parabolic pattern as shown in Figure 3.[24] This proposition holds that the

FIGURE 3. *Defiance*

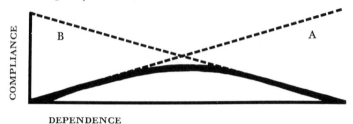

DEPENDENCE

Note: Line A represents motives to comply, while line B represents motives to defy.

most vulnerable dependencies comply at the lower levels expected of considerably less dependent countries as well, and that the greatest compliance is displayed by those whose extent of dependence falls in between.

Now, these first three propositions have been expressed in static terms. They do not speak to the possibility that motivations to comply or defy may change over time. Rather, they share the implicit prediction that a dependency's level of compliance will remain steady, subject to change only if the extent of its dependence also changes with the passage of time. The fourth proposition, however, is explicitly dynamic, attributing changes in a dependency's compliance to temporal shifts in motivational mixes.

DETERIORATING COMPLIANCE

Many writers have proposed that economic dependencies pose a growing problem of control for a dominant state. Although these commentators often emphasize different contributing factors, and while they do not all refer directly to foreign policy concerns, they point toward the behavioral proposition that a dependency's foreign policy accord with that of the dominant state will deteriorate over a period of years.

Spiegel, for one, speaks in very general terms of the growing difficulty that dominant states, in particular the superpowers, have experienced in efforts to control the proliferating numbers of weak, but legally sovereign, countries in the international system of the 1950s and 1960s.[25] He seems to attribute their increasing inability to manipulate these weak states to the emergence of competing, "middle-range" contenders for influence (e.g., Japan, Germany, France, etc.) as well as to the problems inherent in trying to maintain influence over an increasingly large number of dependencies.

Emphasizing internal changes in less-developed countries over the past two or three decades, others would attribute changes in dependencies' foreign policy behavior to phenomena associated with national development. From this domestic perspective, attention is usually paid to the composition of political and economic elites and to the significant influence of the general populace on the policies their leaders pursue. The process of national development produces what Karl Deutsch describes as a "social mobilization" of the populace that may feature "changes of residence, of occupation, of social setting, or face-to-face associates, of institutions, roles, and ways of acting, of experiences and expectations, and finally of personal memories, habits and needs, including the need for new patterns of group affiliation and new images of personal identity. Singly, and even more in their cumulative impact, these changes tend to influence and sometimes to transform political behavior."[26] For such a society, the transformation in politics is, then, a result of new pressures put on their governments by newly mobilized sectors of the populace. In general terms, they will push for political and administrative reform, and for a transformation of the political elite.

Insofar as the newly mobilized populace finds its expectations unsatisfied during its transition to new ways of living and thinking, it will identify targets of its frustration. Its political elites are likely candidates. However, in economically dependent countries, the ruling elites and/or their ascendant political opposition may adroitly deflect blame for socioeconomic failures by identifying foreigners as the root of all evil. (Indeed, it is in this fashion that the intellectual movement against *dependencia* has gained impetus as well as found its political expression.)

Moreover, pinning the blame for economic failure on a malevolent, dominant country is made easier by virtue of the confluence of four phenomena. First, it is objectively true that the dependent economy is extensively penetrated; the charge has much face validity. Additionally, those individuals, firms, and agencies of rich countries that are responsible for the ongoing economics of their dominance have often proven to be insensitive to, or at least ineffectual in dealing with, the poverty of the majority in dependent societies. Third, among those so impoverished are many of the mobilized populace whose poverty combines with a new consciousness that together render them especially responsive to such appeals. Finally, and closely related to social mobilization, has been the elevation of economic and social development to the status of "privileged problems" in less-developed countries; they have become issues that are widely regarded within these societies as highly salient concerns.[27] Thus, there are several complementary reasons associated with changes internal to a dependent society that can prompt its government to comply less and less over time with the dominant state's foreign policy preferences.

By examining the possible effects of dependence over a span of many years, attention can also be given to two further considerations. On the one hand, recall the thesis of numerous analysts of "imperialism" that dependence on trade shifts over time to a dependence on foreign investment,[28] an evolution that may even be accelerated if the dependent state promotes import-substitution industries. Because foreign-owned enterprises in a host country are more visible symbols of dependence than are its own industries engaged in exports and imports, an evolution of dependence away from trade and toward investment can only heighten resentment of the dominant country within the dependent society.[29]

On the other hand, because resentment itself is a psychological phenomenon, the effects of time may be more straightforward. In view of the fact that policymakers are to some extent responsive to the pressures of various domestic constituencies, their motives to defy the wishes of a dominant state have just been suggested to depend considerably upon whether resentment of foreign economic control is widespread among those relevant publics. Consistent with this perspective, then, is the argument that the *spread* of resentment, and its articulated, coherent, politicized *focus* on foreign economic dominance, involve processes that simply require time to unfold. That is, economic dependence may, from the outset, generate resentment within the society, but it is only over a period of years, during which charges and countercharges are exchanged in public and in private, that a broader and more consensual resentment (however well founded) will evolve. By this interpretation, motives of foreign policymakers to defy the dominant state's preferences will be apparent only after the passage of a considerable period of years—and perhaps only after some change of governments transpires. Perusing the history of presumed U.S. hegemony in its hemisphere, Abraham Lowenthal recently observed that "few Latin Americans still assume that their countries' interests and Washington's are inevitably the same; on the contrary, many think that the United States will oppose their concerns, as well as those of the rest of the developing world. Few Latin American leaders now expect U.S.-Latin American relations to be overwhelmingly friendly; most anticipate tensions, if not hostility."[30]

Finally, resentment of economic dependence has also transcended national borders. Nowhere has this been more apparent than in the repeated pressures put on rich countries by the United Nations Conference on Trade and Development (UNCTAD), an organization of about one hundred mostly poor countries. From its beginnings in 1964, UNCTAD has sought to identify and rectify for poor countries perceived injustices in the workings of international economic relations between rich and poor. Among the most significant results of UNCTAD's efforts has been the rapid transformation of the U.N. General Assembly's agenda. Whereas the Assembly's proceedings were once dominated by East-West issues of contention between the cold war blocs, led by the United States and the Soviet Union,[31] that body has in recent years come to debate and vote predominantly upon North-South questions of political economy. Encouraged by their sense of shared injustice, and by their majority voting strength in the General Assembly, the South's poor countries have displayed considerable voting cohesion. Thus, poor economic dependencies may be inspired to defy their dominant partners by the sense of exploitation they find widely shared and collectively voiced in the United Nations.

The behavioral proposition consistent with the above considerations, and shown in Figure 4, holds that a dependency's compliance will decrease over time. However, the linearity of the expected deterioration is not, in fact, a necessary concomitant of the proposition but, instead, just a convenient characterization. Even supposing that the extent of its dependence is constant, which the first three propositions suggested would lead to a steady compliance level, the character of domestic mobilization, elite representation in government, or stimulation by the stance of other less-developed countries may vary in both timing and strength from one dependent country to another. As a

FIGURE 4. *Deteriorating Compliance*

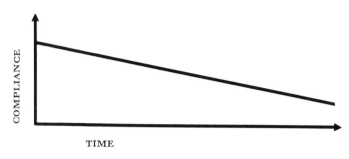

result of one or all of these forces, deteriorating compliance may accelerate over time, as for example a contagion effect among poor countries. Alternatively, declines in compliance may be sporadic, even ratchet-like in appearance, as a government is constituted first of independently willed and then of more submissive elites over the years. (These variant patterns of deterioration can be translated into statistical questions of auto-correlation.)

Regardless of the shape of the downward slope, it bears repeating that this fourth proposition is explicitly temporal in focus, and that it stands in contrast to the stable compliance levels implicit in the preceding static propositions. Of course, all four behavioral expectations intend to reflect the workings of economic forces on political activity. In order to provide a broader perspective and, simultaneously, some further contrast, the following section concludes the theoretical presentation by outlining two alternative, "non-economic" bases for explaining dependencies' foreign policy behavior.

Alternative Explanations

That economic dependence affects a country's foreign policy may be an article of faith to most observers. However, relatively few students would agree that, for dependencies, the history, extent, and makeup of their dependence are the *exclusive* determinants of their external (or, for that matter, their domestic) behavior. What other sorts of factors must also be considered? Depending upon who is asked, answers may be drawn from an enormous range of possibilities, from the organic and psychological drives of the individual to the homeostatic propensities of a global system of nations.

From this range, two "noneconomic" possibilities will be noted. This digression is not merely intended to provide counterbalance to the economic determinants under study, although that alone may be sufficient justification for some. In addition to providing theoretical contrast, or balance, the following may also prove to be useful to the interpretation of empirical materials analyzed later. In service of both of these objectives, the two approaches stem, respectively, from attention to (1) how governments may come to reach decisions and (2) whether nations in geographically defined regions act in ways that distinguish them from other regions.

INCREMENTALISM

In recent years, a number of students of political decision-making have been intrigued by the processes that characterize bureaucracies. It is within large governmental organizations, after all, that scores of people from many divisions and specialized agencies contribute information, analysis, and recommendations to their higher authorities who, in turn, decide what course of action is to be taken. The ways in which these many participants perceive their roles, deal with each other, and impress their superiors are thought to be critically important to an understanding of the resultant behavior of the organization. It should be added that, although on the whole bureaucracies are larger and more numerous in industrial societies, they also are increasingly prominent in the governing of less-developed countries. Consequently, one might reasonably expect bureaucratic behavior of a dependency's foreign ministry. But just what is bureaucratic behavior, and how would it differ from that described by the preceding, economically determined compliance propositions?

In order to address these questions without attempting a lengthy synthesis of a large body of literature, one might consider the well-known "bureaucratic politics paradigm" put forth by Graham Allison.[32] Bureaucrats as institutional representatives are seen as players in a game. Competition among them is based partly on their personal, idiosyncratic backgrounds and styles. But the competition also stems from their respective organizational affiliations, for each of them is motivated to protect the agency, to advance its parochial interests and views, and to act on the basis of information and interpretation that is not held entirely in common with the other players and their organizations. Within the U.S. Military Assistance Program, for example, interrelated government agencies oppose each other in stereotyped fashion. Their competition persists with each of them assuming a policy position that other players can nearly always predict in advance, irrespective of specific personalities or the substance of the issue at hand.[33] The immediate object of the competition is to prevail in shaping the decisions of the superior(s) to whom they are all responsible.

The decision-maker(s) presented by the players with an array of competing recommendations is, of course, operating in the face of considerable uncertainty regarding the final outcome that would follow from any alternative proffered. Thus, the superior is motivated to select or fashion a decision that delays a final accounting, that is, a decision that leaves more time for additional information to be gathered and analyzed.[34] Moreover, a superior is also inclined to develop a compromise that includes pieces of several recommendations received from the competing subordinates. In this way, rewards of the game can be more evenly distributed within the bureaucracy, and thus harmonious working conditions will be favored.

In sum, an emphasis on bureaucratic politics points to the tendency of decision-makers, when supported by the services of large organizations, to take limited action either as a precaution against major errors of commission or as a way in which to compromise the diverse recommendations of subordinates, or both. When a series of such decisions concerning a particular issue is examined over a period of time, it can be described as assuming an incremental form.[35] Thus, any one decision in the series will closely resemble, if not duplicate, the decision that most immediately preceded it. Said differently, the best predictor of the next decision is the one most recently reached.

Because foreign policy decisions are commonly made in consultation with high-level bureaucrats, this perspective offers the proposition that a state's foreign policy behavior on a given issue will change incrementally over time. It provides clear contrast to the more-nearly unitary and rational conception of decision-making implicit in the four dependence-compliance propositions of the preceding section. That is, foreign policy behavior was earlier presented as part of the political economy of exchange between unequals, wherein the dependency calculates the necessity for compliance as a cost weighed against certain economic benefits. Bureaucratic incrementalism, on the other hand, emphasizes the parochialism of fragmented decision-making with its attendant behavioral propensity for more of the same regardless of environmental change.

REGIONALISM

Another way to explain and appraise foreign policy behavior begins with a regional orientation toward international relations. Conventionally, "regions" are geographically defined and include such clusters of nations as sub-Saharan Africa, the Middle East and Northern Africa, Western Europe and Scandinavia, Eastern Europe, Asia, South Asia, Southeast Asia, North America, Central America and the Caribbean, and South America. Depending upon a scholar's purpose and judgment, a geographical "region" may be defined so as to exclude members having "atypical" politics, economics, or culture, such as South Africa and Rhodesia, Israel, Turkey and Greece, New Zealand and Australia, and Haiti, to name a few. Once defined, a regional group of countries can then be considered as either a target of an outsider's foreign policy or as itself an initiator of foreign policy. The following commonplace questions illustrate the implicit assumption that geographical regions are in fact relatively homogeneous:

1. What is Soviet policy toward the Middle East?
   (where the region is a target)

2. How is Latin American policy toward the United States changing?
   (where the region is an initiator)

A different treatment of regions begins not by assuming a priori their existence and analytic utility, but by asking whether geographically proximate groups of countries are indeed sufficiently alike to be lumped together in the first place. Exemplifying this orientation is Bruce Russett's rigorous inquiry covering most national units of the globe of the 1950s and early 1960s.[36] His guiding question was whether, on the basis of national attributes and behavior, geographic clusters could be identified in such a way that differences among members of a group were significantly smaller than differences between that group and other countries or regional groupings. His empirical answer was clearly affirmative, but importantly qualified. The major qualification was that, although there is empirical support for geographical groupings of countries, the list of those to be included as members of a "region" varies according to the types of national attributes or behavior examined. Pakistan, for example, was found to be exactly in the statistical middle of an Afro-Asian grouping of 20 countries for a set of "Catholic culture" variables, whereas it was extremely much less "economically developed" than the others (by two standard deviations from the mean).[37] With respect to external behavior, El Salvador held membership in international organizations in common with most of the Latin American countries from which it nonetheless often voted differently, and was aligned instead with a predominantly Afro-Asian bloc in the General Assembly of the U.N.[38] The reason for mentioning Pakistan and El Salvador is to illustrate Russett's finding that individual members of a region may systematically deviate from other members along one or another dimension of their attributes or behavior patterns.

Nevertheless, it remains demonstrably true that geographical regions of countries *do* tend to manifest similar foreign policy behavior. In this connection, there have been numerous other studies of regionalism in states' roll-call voting behavior in the U.N. General Assembly. The most comprehensive effort of this type remains that of Russett in collaboration with Hayward Alker.[39] Among their many discoveries, only two need to be mentioned here. First, regional voting groups appeared in all four sample years of Assembly voting from the U.N.'s inception through 1961. Second, after the memberships of these regions had been statistically determined, further efforts were made to account for the behavior of "deviants," a label attached to those countries in a *geographical* region that failed to conform to the *behavioral* (voting) propensities of others located in that part of the world.[40] Among Latin American delegations, for example, they found that representatives of authoritarian governments were extensively deviant voters on "East-West" issues whereas, in sharp contrast, the more democratic regimes voted "*always near the middle of the Latin group.*"[41]

But, to return to the broader question, those who focus on regional clusters of nations as initiators of foreign policy activity, whether or not mere geographical proximity is considered a sufficient criterion for group membership, more or less explicitly embrace the proposition that countries of the same region will display similar foreign policy behavior that is distinctively different from that of countries outside the region. Notice that this expectation differs from each of the four propositions that purports to capture the association between foreign policy compliance and economic dependence. An emphasis on regionalism tends to predict homogeneity in foreign policy behavior across a class of countries. Only some of the members of this class may, in fact, be economic dependencies that, according to the dependence thesis, will behave differently from others in the same region.[42]

Alert to the range of possible explanations of foreign policy behavior other than those born of economic dependence, the following chapters report an empirical test of the compliance propositions. As the results of this application unfold, the discussion will occasionally return as well to the questions raised by such foci as bureaucratic incrementalism and regional homogeneity.

Chapter 4
United States Economic Dependencies

This chapter serves two important purposes, both of which are preliminary to the analysis of foreign policy consequences of dependence developed in Chapter 5. The first task here is to identify the countries that were dependent on the United States economy in the period 1950–1973. Second, the patterns of that dependence need to be discussed. For example, is there much variation in the extent to which dependent countries rely on the United States? Does dependence tend to deepen over time? Does investment dependence displace reliance on trade? These patterns provide a contextual map that will be useful later for understanding the foreign policy behavior of the affected countries.

Partly because of a greater availability of pertinent data, the United States and its dependencies are chosen as subjects for study. But a U.S.-dominated group is attractive on other grounds, as well. By most conventional standards, the U.S. possessed greater influence capabilities than any other country during the period of observation. Thus, it should be a revealing example of dominance. Additionally, while the theoretical presentation has been cast in universal language, many of its ideas were originally spawned in the context of U.S. hegemony in the western hemisphere. Examining the adequacy of the dependence framework found in the U.S. context thereby allows some light to be shed on the set of relationships that initially fueled the debate over dependence.

Of course, dependence may be a changing set of relationships rather than a static one. Indeed, underlying most commentaries on contemporary dependence are some dynamic components, most of which ultimately derive from a concern about prospects for national development. Accordingly, it is difficult to quarrel with Patrick McGowan's assessment that time-series indicators are essential in dependence studies.[1] To this end, annual data for the twenty-four years, 1950 through 1973, are included. This time-series format allows trends to emerge in the relationships both within and between variables. In the pages immediately following, the economic variables are specified.

Measuring Economic Dependence

To identify those countries that are asymmetrically dependent on the economy of the United States requires, as a first step, an acquaintance with the measurement procedures adopted in this study. These operations draw on some of the main themes of dependence outlined in Chapter 2. Nevertheless, it is undeniably true that the resultant measures of dependence on trade, investment, and aid can trap only some share of their parent concepts. For example, each indicator can make some claim to reflecting one economy's need for supplies made available by another. In varying degree, however, each is a somewhat less valid measure of the difficulties that would be encountered by an economy that attempts to shift to alternative suppliers. This drawback is partially due to the fact that these economic measures rely on data aggregated to the level of national economies, treating all trade, investment, and aid as identical in kind. Additionally, of course, tapping an actor's *potential*, as, say, in the case of its capability to redirect its external economic relations in the future, is always more difficult than assessing its *actual* relations.

In their defense, on the other hand, some of the virtues of these measures should also be acknowledged. For example, to be a Latin American nation should not be taken as presumptive evidence of economic dependence on the U.S. It would be similarly unconvincing to assert that a country qualifies as a dependency solely because it hosts extensive U.S. private investment, or by virtue of the presence of strong economic ties of all three types in just one "benchmark" year of the twenty-four years under investigation. Instead, dependence is conceived to be a condition of U.S. penetration by several means over a period of years; dependence on the U.S. comes about as a combination of trade, investment, and aid ties over time. As these three economic measures are presented in the following pages, some further attention is given to their reliability and validity in anticipation of substantive interpretations that follow later in this and the next chapter. Finally, each of the three indicants of external dependence is assessed in ratio terms. This step converts into comparable form the estimates of dependence for countries whose domestic economies differ considerably in size and complexity.

A MEASURE OF TRADE DEPENDENCE

Measures of trade dependence (or interdependence) often divide a country's foreign trade by its gross national product (GNP).[2] This ratio is an indication of the extent to which trade is important to a country's economic health.[3] This study uses such an index, but with one modification: only a country's exports appear in the numerator, rather than its total trade (roughly exports plus imports). The decision to use just exports is based on several considerations. First, a reliance on exports should be particularly telling in a less-developed country, since the foreign exchange receipts from its exports are characteristically in very short supply and vital to its attempts to buy capital goods for its economic development. Second, U.S. foreign aid magnifies a recipient's import dependence on U.S. exports because so much of that aid takes the form of tied loans.[4] Because foreign aid is measured separately, leaving import figures in the numerator of the trade ratio would have the undesirable effect of measuring bilateral aid twice. Furthermore, a poor economy tends to export only a few commodities abroad.[5] Thus, the use of only its exports permits the index to tap the vulnerability that is attributed to reliance on a narrow range of exports. Finally, import values usually include the costs of insurance and transportation, items extraneous to the questions at hand; export figures do not.

In sum, trade dependence is measured annually by the following export dependence index (ED):

$$ED_{ij} = a_{ij}/GNP_i,$$

where a_{ij} = the values of country i's exports to country j (the United States);

GNP_i = the gross national product of country i.

The export values are taken principally from various volumes of the United Nations' *Yearbook of International Trade Statistics*.[6] Most of the GNP figures are from United Nations and U.S. Arms Control and Disarmament Agency collections.[7]

A MEASURE OF INVESTMENT DEPENDENCE

Dependence born of foreign investment is a controversial matter. It is almost certainly true that, if more complete data were available, at least some of the existing confusion could be untangled. Nevertheless, the first two chapters offer some general theoretical guidance to measurement. Recall that private foreign investment represents some transfer of valued things such as capital, capital goods, technology, and managerial and labor skills, as well as entailing foreign ownership of means of production. An ideal indicator should therefore incorporate both an estimate of current flows and an estimate of accumulated foreign ownership. Annual *current* flows could be divided by annual domestic capital investment in the host society to produce an approximation of the contribution of the foreign sector to total capital formation for a given year. Similarly, the *accumulated* value of foreign investment could be divided by a figure representing total capital stock on hand in the host economy. But one encounters an insurmountable problem in this last regard because, lamentably, there is no measure of total capital wealth available for most countries, particularly the many poorer ones. Accordingly, foreign investment dependence (ID), as measured here, can only tap current flows of capital, knowledge, and the like.

The formula for this ratio is

$$\text{ID}_t = \frac{(\text{I}_t - \text{I}_{t-1})}{\text{CF}_t},$$

where ID_t = investment dependence for year t
for a host economy;

I_t = the value of United States private direct investment in the host economy for year t;

I_{t-1} = the value of U.S. private direct investment in the host economy for the preceding year;

$$CF_t = \text{gross domestic capital formation in the host economy for year } t.$$

The numerator subtracts the year-end book value of direct private investment by U.S.-based firms in the previous year from its counterpart book value for the current year. This difference measure thus reflects not only *new* investment from the U.S. economy into the host's, but it also accounts for annual depreciation of assets and for reinvestment of profits that are otherwise "undistributed" (where distributed profits are commonly repatriated to the U.S. parent firm and/or as dividends to its stockholders).

The year-end book value data in the numerator are drawn largely from the *Survey of Current Business* and other summaries also published by the U.S. Department of Commerce.[8] Although these sources are the most complete, there remain many host countries for which U.S. investments are not reported in order that investor confidentiality can be preserved. The resultant missing data are, in certain instances, estimated by one or more of the following procedures: (1) dividing into yearly installments reported changes in U.S. investment values for two or more successive years; (2) interpolating U.S. investment values between reported years on the basis of reported changes in total (world) foreign investment series; (3) multiplying total foreign investments by known or estimated U.S. shares of that total. Granting the uncertainty of these procedures, it is reassuring that they usually yield values compatible with those reported by the Department of Commerce, where overlaps occur.

It bears repeating, however, that the resultant estimates for investment dependence are not ideal. The validity of the single ratio is not well established because it excludes accumulated foreign ownership shares in the host's productive investments. It should be added that the values of current flows are not very reliable, not only because some have been estimated by procedures enumerated just above, but because they are originally based on a voluntary sample of reports received by the Department of Commerce. In short, they almost certainly contain appreciable random error.

On the other hand, relatively complete time series for gross domestic capital formation, the denominator, are found in the United Nations' *Yearbook of National Accounts Statistics* (1957–1975).[9] They are converted into U.S. dollars using exchange rates reported mainly in the International Monetary Fund's *International Financial Statistics*.[10]

A MEASURE OF AID DEPENDENCE

Official foreign aid is a capital resource for the recipient more purely than is the case for private investment. U.S. aid flows are used in this study with the understanding that the funds are often loaned only after the recipient has agreed to policy changes that meet with IMF approval. The bilateral aid frequently includes surplus foods, donations for emergency relief, and funds from voluntary relief agencies, programs that are not immediately related to economic development. However, the overwhelming majority of these bilateral funds are earmarked for Export-Import Bank loans and for economic development projects and programs. Thus, as an annual capital transfer, dependence on foreign economic aid can also be usefully expressed in proportion to domestic capital formation to arrive at an aid dependence index (AD):

$$AD_t = \frac{A_t}{CF_t},$$

where AD_t = aid dependence for a recipient economy for year t;

A_t = the value of United States bilateral

economic aid to the recipient economy for year t;

CF_t = gross domestic capital formation in
the recipient economy for year t.

The data base for domestic capital formation has already
been noted, but a few comments regarding U.S. bilateral
aid are in order. First, for most years the annual values
are public, as published by AID.[11] They are reliable. However, the data for 1950 through 1957 are published only in
aggregate groups of years. Happily, these values have been
made available in annual form directly from AID.[12]

U.S. military assistance has been omitted, despite the
case that could be made for its inclusion as a type of "dependence." The decision is based on the observation that
military aid is frequently put to noneconomic purposes,
including national preparedness for external threats and
also for control of domestic violence. To add military aid
to the ratio would complicate cross-national comparisons
by introducing an ingredient having a different non-
economic impact and purpose from one recipient to the
next.

Identifying the Dependent Countries

Each country's dependence on the United States must be
summarized and compared to others in order to determine
the population of dependencies to be singled out for further
study. The paucity of prior empirical work provides no
consensual summary measure of external dependence.
However, since the theoretical underpinnings of dependence emphasize the openness of an economy to foreign
control, it seems reasonable to proceed with an additive
empirical formulation.

The three ratios for dependence on trade, investment,
and aid used here are actually of two types, the difference

reflected in their denominators. The trade ratio divides a country's exports to the U.S. by its GNP, whereas its U.S. aid and private investment figures are expressed in terms of domestic capital formation. At what level is a country "dependent" on another? Marshall Singer suggests a 10 percent threshold for dependence measured by a trade/ GNP ratio which, in turn, translates into a 5 percent criterion here where only exports appear in the numerator.[13] In parallel fashion, the threshold for dependence on foreign capital—aid and investment combined—is set at 10 percent of domestic capital formation. Thus, a dependent country must achieve a minimum total of 15 as the three ratio values are summed for each year.[14]

In application to the time-series data in this study, this partitioning criterion of 15 has been relaxed on intuitive grounds. There is considerable yearly fluctuation in the summary values. If a country were held to the figure of 15 as an *annual* demand, only two countries would qualify as dependencies of the United States.[15] Accordingly, the threshold must be met in at least half of the observed years. Additionally, a country's mean score across those years must at least equal 15.[16]

Table 4 lists the countries that thereby qualify as U.S. economic dependencies, ranked by the degree of their combined dependence. Perhaps the most striking feature of this group is the predominance of Caribbean and Latin American countries, numbering nineteen of the twenty-three dependencies. Their large majority, of course, bears empirical witness to the Latin origins of so much of the *dependencia* criticism leveled at the United States.

Canada is not included as a dependency in this study despite the fact that it meets the criteria of sufficiency and regularity in its combined export and investment relations with the U.S. The grounds for its exclusion, its highly industrial and correspondingly wealthy status, are admittedly not empirical. However, because the theoretical underpinnings of dependence so consistently point to the inequality between dominant and dependent countries' wealth as a precondition to the relationship, the case of the United States and Canada appears to be a very poor fit; Canada is clearly sensitive but it is not likely to be commensurately vulnerable in comparison to the poorer dependencies. By implication, although applicable to just Canada in this study, a third criterion of dependence can now be acknowledged: a necessary condition of (asymmetrical) international dependence is economic inequality, as a difference in national attributes.[17]

The absence of Argentina, Brazil, and Mexico from the dependent population is conspicuous and deserves comment. Perhaps because of their greater size, these countries—especially Brazil—are among the favorite examples of dependence pointed to in the case study literature.[18] However, the economics of dependence surveyed in Chapter 2 draw attention to the vulnerability of *poor* and *small* economies. In this context, a comparison with Venezuela, the largest and wealthiest of the dependencies listed above, is instructive. In per capita terms, Argentina, Brazil, and Mexico are not as wealthy as Venezuela, which marginally qualifies as a dependency in this study. However, their economies in 1965, for example, are two and three times larger in absolute (GNP) terms than even Venezuela's.[19] In short, despite Venezuela's oil wealth, the absence of these three large, industrializing Latin economies is consistent with the theoretical expectation that the poorest of the poor are the most susceptible to economic penetration. By these measures, in fact, Mexico never qualifies as a U.S. dependency after 1958, Brazil never qualifies after 1961 (and only twice before that, in 1956–1957), and Argentina qualifies in *none* of the two dozen years scrutinized.[20]

Other notable characteristics of this population are the wide range and varying compositions of dependence score averages.[21] Panama, averaging a staggering 81.1, is by far the most dependent among them, principally owing of

Table 4. *Dependencies of the United States, 1950–1973*

| Country | Dependence Averages[a] | | | |
	ED	ID	AD	Sum
Panama	5.6	62.3	13.2	81.1
Bolivia	14.4	8.0	33.6	56.0
Liberia	20.0	14.6	20.8	55.4
Jamaica	9.7	30.9	4.0	44.6
China, Taiwan	2.8	1.7	40.0	44.5
Dominican Republic	12.2	4.2	14.7	31.1
Honduras	12.6	9.1	7.9	29.6
Trinidad/Tobago	26.5	....	2.1	28.6
Nicaragua	7.1	5.9	14.0	27.0
Cuba	17.6	7.5	1.1	26.2
Costa Rica	11.5	4.2	7.8	23.5
Guyana	12.8	....	9.5	22.3
Haiti	6.2	3.3	12.6	22.1
El Salvador	9.7	2.4	9.0	21.1
Guatemala	6.5	4.1	10.2	20.8
Indonesia	1.8	3.6	14.3	19.7
Venezuela	12.4	4.8	1.7	18.9
Ecuador	6.7	3.3	8.6	18.6
Paraguay	2.4	2.1	13.3	17.8
Peru	6.0	5.5	5.6	17.1
Philippines	5.9	2.4	8.5	16.8
Chile	2.7	3.5	10.2	16.4
Colombia	6.9	2.8	6.6	16.3

[a] .... signifies that no data are available.

[b] These totals may include years in which only one or two of the three ratios could be calculated on the basis of the evidence available

[c] Relevant years are those in which a country exists as a separate political entity.

course to the extraordinary and continuous quantities of new private investment capital pumped into operations associated with the Canal Zone. Bolivia, the second-most dependent, is heavily reliant on trade and aid relations with the U.S. And the dependence of third-highest Liberia is rather evenly spread across all three categories. In fact, there is a similar diversity throughout the list, with some countries' dependence mainly attributable to just one form of economic reliance while, for others, penetration is more evenly distributed. The one exception to this diversity is discovered at the lower end of the ranking where foreign investment dependence is nowhere a prominent contributor to the summary scores.

Table 4 does not report the annual values, but inter-country differences do stand out across years, as well as across types of dependence. For example, Peru, the Philippines, and Venezuela achieve the threshold score 15 more often in the 1950s, while Ecuador, El Salvador, and Indonesia are more dependent in later years. There are also cases where the extent of a country's dependence is relatively invariant across time, including high-ranked Bolivia and low-ranked Chile (at least until the Allende period). However, in keeping with the aggregate decline of Latin American economic ties to the U.S. by the late 1960s, there is some tendency for dependence scores to decline, on balance, over the study period (see Figure 5).

With respect to the identity of these dependent countries, two final comments are warranted. First, there are probably a few additional countries that would qualify if more complete data were available for them. Among them might be Jordan, Nepal, Thailand, and Uganda, for which few trade data and no private investment data are at hand. Indeed, it is probably accurate to say that this population of twenty-three dependencies overemphasizes Latin America, where data are somewhat more accessible than elsewhere in the Third World. Second, it should be noted at the outset of the empirical portion of this study that most of the statistical analyses hereafter treat each country as a separate case. This has the virtue of allowing the reader to ignore results for those countries that may seem not to be appropriate for inclusion in the first place. (Alas, there is no way to *add* countries except by collecting and analyzing the data oneself!)

As an operational procedure, the qualifications of a "dependent" country are entirely empirical rather than a priori regionally defined. Furthermore, dependence is three-pronged in its measure, and thereby more sensitive to changes that are proposed to have political consequences than a narrower instrument would be. Finally, the criteria for dependent status include the need for at least a modicum of consistency over many years. If these standards seem too strict, excluding countries inappropriately, it can be said in reply that these demands should only highlight differences between the present set of dependencies and other countries. In short, high standards of economic dependence will provide a stronger inferential basis regarding the foreign policy consequences that this study ultimately addresses.

The Instability of Dependence

Since, to qualify as a dependency, a country must meet a threshold value with some consistency, one might reasonably presume that the dependence scores of the population would therefore display stability over time. Figure 5 offers information in this connection, showing dependence score averages for the twenty-three countries from 1950 through 1973. In fact, there are appreciable oscillations from year to year in the average dependence of the group. With a range of about ± 25 percent from the grand mean of 29.2, several years witness changes of 20 percent from the pre-

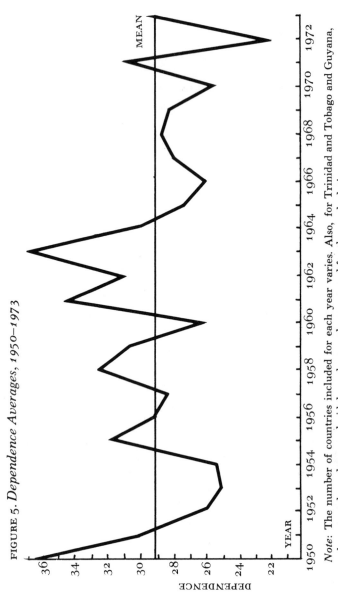

FIGURE 5. *Dependence Averages, 1950–1973*

Note: The number of countries included for each year varies. Also, for Trinidad and Tobago and Guyana, only export dependence and aid dependence values are used for these calculations.

ceding twelve-month value. Additionally, the figure reveals a discernible decline following the high points of the early 1960s, even though annual fluctuations persist.[22]

Now, dependence theorists predict that extensive penetration into a poor economy, once under way, is self-perpetuating. In the light of the fluctuating averages just observed, one might wonder whether these variations for the twenty-three countries are largely attributable to changes experienced by just a few among them. In particular, it is arithmetically possible that the most dependent countries in the group have a disturbing impact on the stable majority whose scores are consistently lower.

To test this possibility and the more general proposition of stable dependence, each dependency has been analyzed individually. By plotting a country's dependence score for each year against its score for the previous year, a set of observations is derived. Each set is then summarized by a coefficient, R^2, which indicates the extent to which successive observations follow a linear path through time. These statistics are reported in Table 5, showing that yearly fluctuations of dependence are indeed ubiquitous among the group members. Furthermore, as they are listed again by rank, there is no apparent difference between highly dependent countries and those with lower averages.[23] Are these fluctuations simply the result of unreliable investment data? Apparently not, for the results hardly differ if one looks at total dependence (column 1), aid and investment dependence (column 2), or export and aid dependence (column 3). Perhaps the instability arises instead from price changes for exported primary goods. If so, then one would not predict the results in column 4, where export dependence, taken alone, proves to be more stable than the other series. (Column 4 has been calculated in only a few cases where other series are considerably shorter.)

A more graphic version of these widespread fluctuations is shown in Figure 6. Here, with four representative countries, the content of unstable dependence is more readily

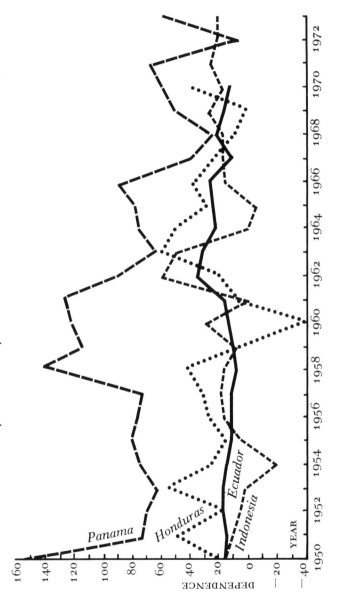

FIGURE 6. Four Cases of Unstable Dependence

grasped. In this sample, only Ecuador follows a very consistent pattern and, even there, one sees a few fluctuations amounting to some 10 or 20 points in adjacent years. In absolute terms, Panama experiences the greatest changes, but its much greater levels of dependence dampen the statistical effect of those oscillations.

On the basis of these data, the obvious conclusion is that the level of a country's dependence on the United States is subject to dramatic reversals from one year to the next. But this fact does not warrant the statement that, as a corollary, dependence varies widely around a *steady* level through time. In truth, this is not empirically correct. Recall, for example, that the group average was already seen to decline (see Figure 5). For further illumination, consider the individual countries plotted in Figure 7. Here are three cases of clear secular decline, and each grows less dependent for different reasons. In the case of Venezuela, the ratio of new private investment to domestic capital formation declines precipitously after 1960, with negative values for most of the remaining years because of both net depreciation and eventual nationalization of foreign oil holdings. Starting in the mid-1960s, its export dependence also declines from 14 percent of the GNP to just 5.4 percent in 1973. For the Philippines, on the other hand, reductions in dependence in the last decade are exclusively at the hands of the private investment sector. Yet a different configuration accounts for the decline in Nationalist China's dependence. There, trade and investment ties to the U.S. economy actually increase through the mid-1960s, only to be outweighed by huge decreases in bilateral aid. In sum, the falling dependence for these three countries represents various mixtures of the economic factors and parallels the group trend noted earlier.

Not surprisingly, there are a few countries for which dependence increases over time, in contrast to the group trend. Three, in particular, stand out. Dependence in the Dominican Republic scores much higher in the 1960s than

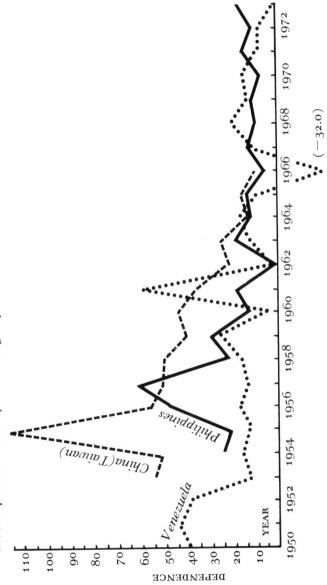

FIGURE 7. *Three Cases of Decreasing Dependence*

in the previous decade, with the trend mainly attributable to Alliance for Progress foreign aid and, secondarily, to private investment. In El Salvador, these same two factors increase in approximately equal measure. And, in Trinidad and Tobago, where investment data are not in the public record, reliance on exports to the U.S. accounts for the doubling of its score since its political independence in 1961.

What, then, can be said to characterize the combined dependence of this population over a period of twenty-four years? First, it is clear that their dependence scores display marked annual changes, both for the group average and for almost all of them treated individually. It is also true that their group average shows some decline in the second half of the study period. Finally, however, there is a rather full range of diversity in their individual patterns. For some, dependence follows the group average downward. For others, reliance on the U.S. economy increases. And for many of them, dependence oscillates around a more steady mean. Thus, both the individual and collective patterns are to some extent at odds with the proposition that dependence, once established, is a stable condition.

A closely related assertion found in the dependence literature holds that breaking away from economic subservience is nearly impossible. In light of the present evidence, this point is even more arguable than the stability assertion. Both Brazil and Mexico, for example, move away from dependence in the early years, and hence fail to qualify for inclusion in this study's population of dependencies. Among those that do qualify, several countries experience secular declines, even to the point that Chile, Peru, the Philippines, and Venezuela do not once meet the dependence threshold criterion in the last five to ten years of the study period.[24] In short, dependence on the United States can be reduced and even escaped, contrary to a common assumption.

This mixture raises the question whether countries that successfully reduce their economic reliance on the U.S. differ systematically in other relevant respects from those that maintain their dependence. For example, one might reasonably wonder whether the former are able to reduce their dependence because it starts at a lower level. Particularly in view of the uncertainty of an empirical threshold for dependence in the first place, it may seem reasonable to suppose that *self-perpetuating* dependence is most probable among the most highly penetrated of the dependencies.

Table 6 separates the dependencies into subsets according to whether their respective vulnerabilities noticeably decrease. Mexico and Brazil are added to the list here, since they were earlier seen to be prime examples of countries that came to escape dependence on the United States. A look at the mean first-year dependence scores flatly contradicts the guiding supposition; the economic dependence average for the first year among the "diminishing" countries is 41.6 whereas it is only 22.2 for those with constant or increasing dependence.

This comparison, however, only triggers further speculation. Recall from Chapter 2 that a poor economy may consciously choose the high-risk strategy that entails greater short-run dependence in order to attempt long-run economic development and, as a by-product, the ultimate withering of its need for external supplies. If this thesis has merit, then perhaps the difference between "diminishing" and "constant" dependencies is attributable to the former groups' adoption of the high-risk option. The logic of the argument, after all, implies exactly the empirical manifestations just observed, namely, especially high initial dependence followed some years later by marked declines that may finally break the economic shackles (as for Mexico and Brazil in the 1950s and Peru and the Philippines in the 1960s). If such a process actually underlies the subgroup difference above, then the attendant economic devel-

Table 6. *Initial Dependence for
Two Subgroups of Dependencies*

Country	Dependence Value for Initial Year	
Diminishing dependence		
Mexico	13.2	(1952)
Brazil	8.7	(1950)
Panama	162.9	(1950)
Jamaica	42.5	(1967)
China, Taiwan	42.4	(1960)
Costa Rica	23.7	(1950)
Venezuela	23.1	(1954)
Peru	13.5	(1950)
Philippines	44.1	(1951)
Average Dependence	41.6	
Constant dependence		
Bolivia	49.8	(1950)
Liberia	35.2	(1967)
Dominican Republic	20.0	(1950)
Honduras	20.2	(1950)
Trinidad/Tobago[a]	22.5	(1962)
Nicaragua	17.1	(1958)
Cuba	28.7	(1951)
Guyana[a]	26.2	(1966)
Haiti	14.7	(1953)
El Salvador	12.3	(1958)
Guatemala	20.7	(1950)
Indonesia	21.4	(1958)
Ecuador	14.0	(1950)
Paraguay	17.2	(1960)
Chile	19.6	(1950)
Colombia	14.8	(1950)
Average Dependence	22.2	

[a] Initial values for these countries include just export and aid dependence.

opment achieved by higher short-run dependence should itself be apparent.

To probe this possibility, the per capita GNPs of the subgroups are compared in Table 7, together with their unstandardized national products. In conjunction with the preceding table, the present per person production data yield two significant conclusions. First, despite their higher initial dependence, the countries that experience diminishing U.S. penetration are generally much more developed than those in the constant category, and this difference persists as early as 1950. On the other hand, the rate of per capita growth in their respective economies is, within the range of probable measurement error, identical. Thus, diminishing dependence is not accompanied by a more rapid rate of economic development that itself might be expected to result from higher dependence in the early years, even though the level of that development is higher.

Finally, the absolute (GNP) size of the economies in the two groups may be important. As Mexico, Brazil, and Argentina were first discussed, it was pointed out that their economies are simply much larger than those of their dependent Latin counterparts. In the present, broader comparison of national products, one quickly sees that the subgroup of countries with the higher initial dependence average, the "diminishing" set, also features a mean economic size more than twice that of the others in 1950. Moreover, as the first countries experience declining dependence on the United States in the following twenty-three years, the size of their economies simultaneously grows much faster than is true for countries where dependence is steady or increasing.

This brief digression suggests that there are indeed pertinent differences between countries that move away from dependence and those that do not. First, the former are more heavily reliant in the early years observed. However, they also have larger and more developed economies,

Table 7. *Economic Development and Economic Size for Two Subgroups of Dependencies*

Country	GNP Per Capita ($U.S.)		GNP (U.S. $ millions)		Growth Rate (annual %) GNP/	
	1950	1973	1950	1973	Cap	GNP
Diminishing Dependence						
Mexico	186	745	4,699	43,272		
Brazil	264	595	13,765	62,042		
Panama	306	994	245	1,591		
China, Taiwan	128e	373e	998e	10,200		
Costa Rica	290	708	232	1,346		
Venezuela	589	1,524	2,888	17,674		
Peru	121	596	1,013	9,182		
Philippines	168	262	3,288	10,860		
Average:	256	725	3,419	19,520	7.6	20.5
Constant dependence						
Bolivia	60	162	248	874		
Dominican Republic	152	485	349	2,233		
Honduras	137	334	205	869		
Nicaragua	122	547	147	1,094		
Haiti	87	126	277	565		
El Salvador	154	314	338	1,258		
Guatemala	222	476	621	2,474		
Indonesia	120e	98	8,820e	12,545		
Ecuador	152	365	471	2,552		
Paraguay	124	377	174	981		
Chile	374	1,376	2,167	13,898		
Colombia	183	419	2,049	10,066		
Average:	157	423	1,322	4,117	7.4	9.2

Note: To maintain cohort group comparisons, certain dependencies are deleted from these calculations. (They are Jamaica, Liberia, Trinidad and Tobago, Cuba, and Guyana.) All values are expressed in current dollars, thereby inflating differences between 1950 and 1973.

e: estimate based on extrapolation using rate of change reported for 1950 in Bruce M. Russett et al., *World Handbook of Political and Social Indicators* (New Haven: Yale University Press, 1964); rates for 1973 are taken from Charles Lewis Taylor and Michael C. Hudson, *World Handbook of Political and Social Indicators*, 2nd ed. (New Haven: Yale University Press, 1972).

and their absolute size grows at about twice the rate of the others. In short, larger and more developed economies enjoy better prospects of reducing or escaping dependence. This last pattern was anticipated in Chapter 2, where theoretical considerations pointed to the likelihood that a dependent syndrome is more easily maintained when the partner is small and poor.

A "New Dependence"?

Another assertion states that historical dependence on trade has been displaced by a "new dependence" on foreign capital supplied by aid and investment transfers. As noted in Chapter 2, such an evolution is consistent with an additive conception of the three modes of dependence. However, the displacement of trade by capital dependence appears to conflict with the numerous theoretical bases for viewing trade, investment, and aid ties as mutually reinforcing.

Strictly speaking, capital displacement implies that a dependency's reliance on trade declines at the same time its investment and aid links grow stronger. That is, trade and capital are proposed to have an inverse association. A look at the interrelations among the three dimensions of economic dependence provides a preliminary assessment. The operational procedure simply regresses a country's export dependence on the sum of its investment and aid dependence according to the equation

$$ED_t = a + b \ (ID_t + AD_t).$$

The displacement proposition thereby translates into the hypothesis that the regression coefficient for capital ($ID_t + AD_t$) is a negative value.

The first three columns of Table 8 report the statistical results for this equation, while the fourth through seventh columns show coefficients from a parallel regression equa-

Table 8. *Coefficients of Capital Displacement*

Country	Capital	(t)	R
Panama	− .02	(−1.80)	.12
Bolivia	− .17	(−2.29)	.23
Liberia	− .02	(− .60)	.06
Jamaica	−0.00	(−5.84)	.00
China, Taiwan	−0.00	(−4.39)	.70
Dominican Republic	.01	(.34)	.00
Honduras	.03	(.69)	.02
Trinidad/Tobago			.54
Nicaragua	0.00	(.13)	.00
Cuba	− .03	(− .23)	.00
Costa Rica	− .14	(−1.89)	.15
Guyana			.00
Haiti	− .02	(− .73)	.05
El Salvador	− .08	(−1.33)	.13
Guatemala	− .05	(−1.83)	.15
Indonesia	− .01	(− .69)	.03
Venezuela	.05	(1.60)	.12
Ecuador	− .03	(− .97)	.04
Paraguay	.02	(.56)	.03
Peru	− .01	(− .14)	.00
Philippines	− .01	(− .47)	.01
Chile	.03	(.84)	.03
Colombia	− .24	(−2.15)	.17

Note: Main values in Capital, Investment, and Aid columns are
weights; values in parentheses are *t*-test statistics. In subsec
equations and tables, b symbolizes beta weight.

tion where investment and aid dependence are disaggregated into separate factors. These latter coefficients are presented only in order to see more clearly to which factors
the main results should be attributed.

Including Guyana and Trinidad and Tobago, for which
there are no investment data, seventeen of the twenty-

Investment	(t)	Aid	(t)
− .01	(−1.64)	0.00	(7.19)
− .41	(−1.57)	− .12	(−1.21)
− .02	(− .26)	.11	(.76)
−0.00	(− .03)	− .11	(− .30)
.06	(.45)	− .03	(−4.25)
.04	(1.24)	−0.00	(− .15)
.02	(.57)	.05	(.45)
		−2.04	(−3.48)
.01	(.09)	0.00	(.08)
− .03	(− .75)	1.27	(6.38)
− .06	(− .86)	− .38	(−2.80)
		− .01	(− .13)
− .06	(− .79)	− .01	(− .28)
−1.00	(−5.04)	− .01	(− .27)
− .04	(− .68)	− .07	(−1.21)
.05	(1.75)	− .03	(−2.00)
− .06	(−1.71)	− .38	(−1.15)
− .21	(−4.53)	.01	(.42)
− .08	(− .49)	.02	(.63)
− .02	(− .57)	.12	(1.64)
− .12	(−1.73)	.01	(.44)
− .05	(−1.20)	.16	(3.03)
− .06	(− .41)	− .32	(−2.75)

three depedencies show negative capital coefficients in relation to changes in export dependence. Additionally, one
could reason that broad, historical processes cannot be presumed to follow closely, year-in and year-out, their long-
run trends. Thus, one could overlook the low R^2 values
that represent wide scatters around the average relation-

ship between capital and export dependence. The results of this test might be taken as corroboration of the capital dependence hypothesis were it not for three considerations that mitigate the initial impression.

First, while the negative signs are supportive, the substantive interpretation applicable to most of these seventeen cases is that the average rate of capital displacement is negligible. Second, the t-test statistics indicate that, for about half of those with negative estimates, there is a good chance that the true association between capital and export dependence is zero or slightly positive. Finally, the negative slope for Trinidad and Tobago is due to increasing trade ties in tandem with decreasing capital flows (here, just foreign aid), a trend exactly *opposite* that predicted by capital displacement. As a result, only Bolivia, Costa Rica, and Colombia show the appreciable and reliably inverse relationship hypothesized. In short, the initial impression of corroboration given by Table 8 is vitiated upon closer examination.

However, a variant of the displacement proposition specifies a somewhat different relation between trade and capital dependence and may thereby permit its survival despite these first results. It is entirely possible that the historical pattern is not so much one of displacement but one instead of capital as a *supplement* to trade. In other words, an alternative possibility is that the ties of trade may retain their strength in absolute terms, only to be *relatively* diminished by rising investment and aid flows. Compared to displacement, this second pattern of capital expansion would be more in line with theoretical statements positing that trade, investment, and aid relations stimulate each other's perpetuation. And it seems more in keeping with the dependence profiles reviewed earlier, wherein the impression was one of variety in these interrelations.

In order to convert this second interpretation into a form that can be more systematically tested, procedural steps must admit three possible relations between trade and capital as supportive evidence. Capital dependence can increase relative to trade dependence if (1) trade declines while capital flows decline more slowly, are stable, or increase; (2) trade is stable while capital flows increase; (3) trade increases while capital flows increase faster. In other words, the ratio of capital dependence to trade dependence is hypothesized to increase over time, rather than to stay constant or decrease. Table 9 subdivides the dependencies according to whether a visual inspection of the annual ratio values conforms to this exception.

For only nine of the dependencies does capital increase relative to trade dependence, and for six others there is a trend in the opposite direction. Further, the most marked changes in this ratio are also distributed rather evenly between the first and third subgroups. Now, because the "new dependence" on capital corresponds in principle to import-substitution policies, some additional features of the table are interesting. Notice, for example, that changes in all three modes of dependence occur with regularity as the capital-to-trade balance shifts in either direction. Thus, among both the first nine and the last six countries, the three dependence indices share roughly equal responsibility for the larger patterns. In the first group, then, the mixture of factors strongly resembles the "new dependence" picture. However, one could argue that foreign aid pumped into Latin America through the Alliance for Progress in the early and mid-1960s is historically specific. That is, six of the nine supportive cases partially owe their increasing capital ratio to an accident of the spatial and temporal domains of the evidence; in another setting there might well be even less support forthcoming for the "new dependence." Of course, even nine cases are unpersuasive as prima facie documentation.

From another perspective, there is even further reason to question the strength of these results. Recalling that

Table 9. *Changing Ratios of Capital Dependence to Export Dependence*

Country	Change Attributable To: ED	ID	AD	Diminishing Dependence
Increasing Ratio				
Bolivia	X	X		
LIBERIA		X		
Dominican Republic			X	
NICARAGUA		X	X	
Costa Rica		X	X	X
EL SALVADOR	X	X	X	
Guatemala	X	X		
ECUADOR	X	X		
COLOMBIA	X		X	
Steady Ratio				
Jamaica				X
Honduras				
Cuba				
Guyana				
Haiti				
Indonesia				
Paraguay				
Peru				X
Decreasing Ratio				
PANAMA		X		X
CHINA, TAIWAN	X		X	X
Trinidad/Tobago[a]	X		X	
Venezuela		X		X
Philippines		X	X	X
CHILE		X		

Note: Country names in capital letters denote stronger increasing and decreasing trends.

[a] Investment data are not available.

seven of these economies experience diminishing total dependence and relatively faster growth at a steadily higher plane of development, one would logically expect them to appear among the first group in Table 9. The rationale for this expectation is simply that the high-risk strategy presumed to underlie eventual diminution of dependence includes inducements to private foreign investors and assumptions of extensive foreign aid loans, measures that should also reduce the need for export earnings. Or to put the matter differently, one might look at the first three columns of Table 9 and reason that the first nine countries were following such a strategy and therefore could be expected to enjoy diminishing dependence on the U.S. The fourth column shows this not to be true. Indeed, the "diminishing" countries tend to fall into the third group where trade dependence increases relative to capital dependence, even as their total dependence declines.

Summary

The emergent picture of economic dependence on the United States is therefore more complex than is frequently presumed.[25] Not only does the extent of dependence vary from one country to the next, it is especially subject to change under certain combinations of conditions. The empirical materials brought to bear on several dependence propositions offer support for some while casting serious doubt on others. The following paragraphs itemize the most germane of these findings.

1. *Most U.S. dependencies are Caribbean and Latin American countries.* Nineteen of the twenty-three countries included in the dependent population are located in the western hemisphere. If data were more fully accessible, a few additional nonwestern economies might well qualify. Nev-

ertheless, this geographical concentration is consistent with previous research and common speculation.

2. *The extent of U.S. economic penetration varies enormously among these dependent countries.* In terms of individual country averages, first-ranked Panama is five times more dependent than last-ranked Colombia.

3. *Dependence on the U.S. declines in the last decade under study.* This is true for the dependent group as a whole, and, despite a few contrary cases, it is also true for a substantial number of individual countries. The unqualified assertion that external dependence is self-perpetuating is therefore oversimplified.

4. *Dependence scores fluctuate greatly in successive years.* Dramatic annual shifts characterize both the group average and virtually all individual dependencies. In combination with item 3 (above), there are clear signals that the dominance-dependence phenomenon is unstable, even though this instability is at least implicitly denied by many commentators.[26]

5. *Some conditions appear to increase the likelihood that a country can eventually escape its dependence.* Secular declines in dependence are associated with greater economic development and larger absolute size, in keeping with theoretical expectations.

6. *Capital dependence does not uniformly displace or outdistance trade dependence over time.* Most surprising here is the discovery that the "new dependence" on capital is most likely among dependencies whose ties to the United States are relatively constant or even increasing, the very countries featuring lower economic development and smaller size. In other words, capital dependence does not

materialize as a manifestation of the high-risk development strategy as is often supposed.

With regard to these summary points, it is important to enter a disclaimer. This chapter does not purport to scrutinize closely the developmental effects of foreign dominance even though the flourishing interest in *dependencia* regards questions of economic growth as paramount.[27] Rather, the purpose served by analyzing in some detail these ties between the United States and its dependencies is to set the stage for testing the foreign policy consequences presumed to result from economic dependence. The next chapter investigates the foreign policy propositions against this economic backdrop.

Chapter 5
Compliance in the
General Assembly

Armed now with a sense of the texture and change of economic dependence, one can turn to the political consequences toward which the study has been aimed. Is there a linear and positive relationship between the extent of a country's dependence on the United States and the degree to which it complies with the foreign policy preferences of the North American giant, or do diminishing marginal political gains for the U.S. set in instead? Is there a political backlash when dependence worsens? Does foreign policy compliance deteriorate with the passage of time? These and other questions can be tested only if comparisons are drawn between the foreign policy behavior of the dependencies and the behavior of other countries not reliant on economic supplies from the United States. But before the propositions can be tested, the political data base must be described.

Measuring Compliance

Systematic and quantitative measures of political behavior are often elusive and contentious. Foreign policy is no exception. Therefore, following numerous precedents, foreign policy behavior is measured in this study in terms of votes in the United Nations General Assembly. This choice is recommended by several considerations.

First, in response to expectations that the foreign policy behavior of dependencies should somehow be distinctive in the international arena, one is forced to look somewhere for visible evidence. Governments have a variety of means to bestow political exchanges. Unfortunately, the publicity and frequency of such occasions vary so greatly among countries in the contemporary world that they are difficult to specify in a systematic, comparative, and comprehensive fashion.[1] By contrast, votes in some international organizations are regular and public statements of the member governments through their delegates.[2] Among international organizations, the U.N. General Assembly seems appropriate to this study owing to its almost universal membership, a feature that maximizes the number of countries for which a measure can be constructed for an extended number of years.

Second, analysts of the U.N. suggest that politics in the General Assembly mirror international economic dependence. Inis Claude contends in this regard that "the major states have at least as much influence within and upon [the Assembly] as they are entitled to, by virtue of their size, strength, and general importance."[3] Robert Keohane identifies economic dependence even more explicitly as an important motive for roll call agreement: "The more dependent a state is on a great power for trade, aid, or protection, the more responsive it is likely to be to pressure [in the Assembly]."[4] It therefore seems useful and appropriate to employ U.N. votes to test the foreign policy consequences of economic dependence.

A third reason for choosing Assembly roll call votes as an indicator of dependencies' foreign policy rests on two aspects of the international environment of dependent states. On the one hand, international organizations in general, and the U.N. in particular, represent the only viable arenas in which many poor countries are able to express their political views publicly.[5] In addition, participation in international organizations by such states is very often motivated by economic considerations.[6] This latter characteristic makes the U.N. an especially appropriate setting for the observation of dependencies.

Finally, the reasoning of Karl Deutsch is reassuring. He suggests that influence exerted and compliance extended are often opposite sides of the same coin. Speaking to this conception of influence/compliance, he says: "The weight of the power or influence of an actor over some process is the extent to which he can change the probability of its outcome. This can be measured most easily wherever we are dealing with a repetitive class of similar outcomes, such as votes in the United Nations Assembly."[7]

For these reasons, political compliance is operationally defined in a manner that captures the extent of expected behavior on the part of dependencies relative to the unexpected. Using Arend Lijphart's Index of Agreement (IA), the accord among Assembly roll call positions for a pair of nations over a series of votes can be summarized.[8] Lijphart's index is

$$IA = [f + 1/2\ g]/t,$$

where f = number of votes on which the pair agrees (Yes-Yes, Abstain-Abstain, No-No);

g = number of votes on which that pair partially agrees (Yes-Abstain, No-Abstain);

t = total number of votes on which the pair voted.

General Assembly voting annually covers a very wide range of substantive issues. It would be most surprising to discover that any country attempts to exert influence over others across the issue spectrum. Rather, it must be conceded that a member nation attaches to only some voting outcomes any importance worthy of mention. Accordingly, the intervening concept of *issue salience* is introduced to distinguish between those roll calls that are likely to prompt the United States to search out voting allies and those resolutions that are seldom, if ever, salient to the U.S.[9] Of immediate interest, of course, is the voting behavior of the twenty-three dependencies. It is presumed in this regard that they are among the obvious targets of U.S. influence attempts on issues the latter finds salient. In short, political behavior can be part of a political-economic exchange only when that behavior is of value to its recipient. Therefore, only those roll calls that are salient to the United States should be used to test propositions regarding its political influence.

Between 1950 and 1973, there has surely been no set of issues consistently more important to the United States than those bearing on its cold war with the Soviet Union.[10] Despite the détente of recent years, a continuous stream of events signals the continuing salience to the U.S. of superpower antagonisms. Hardly a major U.S. foreign policy decision seems to be reached without considering its implications for relations with the leader of the communist camp. For example, President Carter's first nominee to direct the Central Intelligence Agency met stiffer Senate opposition than did the President's choice to head the negotiating team for strategic arms talks; the latter was approved. But both men came under heavy attack in some quarters on grounds that they might not be sufficiently vigilant in the face of a continuing Soviet threat to U.S. security. Former Secretary of State Kissinger, testifying before the Senate Foreign Relations Committee in 1973, stated that the cold war interests of the United States far outweigh economic questions.[11] Thus, because cold war issues are of great salience to the U.S., Assembly votes on superpower contests should be the occasions on which dependencies' positions are of theoretical interest.

Following this logic, the roll calls are partitioned into

two categories, "Cold War" and "Others." The partitioning rule is simple: when the United States and the Soviet Union take positions in complete disagreement, the roll call is assigned to the "Cold War" category.[12] "Others" is the residual designation for votes in which the bloc leaders are in agreement or partial agreement, or else in which the Soviet Union does not vote and the United States does. (If the U.S. does not vote, the roll call is discarded, having no value in computing IAs with the U.S.)

The Index of Agreement scores require three types of information: (1) the total number of roll calls in which both countries vote, for each pair; (2) the number of votes with ballot agreement; (3) the number of votes with partial agreement. Assembly roll calls that receive at least 90 percent agreement as well as resolutions that are voted on paragraph-by-paragraph are excluded because they provide virtually no additional information about delegate preferences.[13] The raw data from which this information is derived are from the International Relations Archive of the Inter-University Consortium for Political and Social Research.[14]

An Overview of Assembly Voting

As a backdrop to the four compliance propositions to be tested below, it is useful to begin with some descriptive voting information. To this end, group averages of agreement with the United States are illustrated in Figures 8 and 9.

The first of these two graphs compares the dependent group to all other Assembly voters on Cold War issues.[15] One clear impression is that the group differences are quite distinct, with the dependencies in greater accord with U.S. Cold War positions. One-way analysis of variance confirms this picture: in eleven of the fourteen sessions between

1955 and 1969,[16] the group differences are not at all likely the result of chance ($p < .05$). Even though the differences in early and late sessions are less marked, their direction is entirely consistent with the middle period. The second point of interest here is the marked decline in support for the U.S. from both groups, starting in the mid-1960s.

The parallel comparison in Figure 9 takes on added meaning in the context of these patterns. Here, where votes on Other issues are examined instead, once again both groups increasingly diverge from the United States in the second decade. However, quite differently this time, the two groups' average scores are remarkably similar. Just seven scattered years show statistically significant differences, and in two of those cases (1972 and 1973) the dependencies more often *disagree* with the U.S. than do the remaining voters.

In sum, the United States experiences dwindling support on both types of issues among both groups of countries beginning in the 1960s.[17] In addition, and more interesting in theoretical terms, are the clear indications that it is meaningful to partition the roll calls according to their salience to the U.S. For, not only do the dependencies average distinctly higher accord with their dominant partner on Cold War issues, but they seldom fail to differ during those same years from other delegates on Other issues (except as they disagree more in late years), also as predicted by the salience concept. However, this overview of prominent voting patterns cannot demonstrate that the agreement of the dependencies with U.S. Cold War positions represents economically motivated political compliance. Instead, it only sets the stage for testing the four political economy propositions that assert such a connection. However, these first comparisons justify using "compliance" as a convenient, if provisional, reference to the Cold War voting of the dependencies.

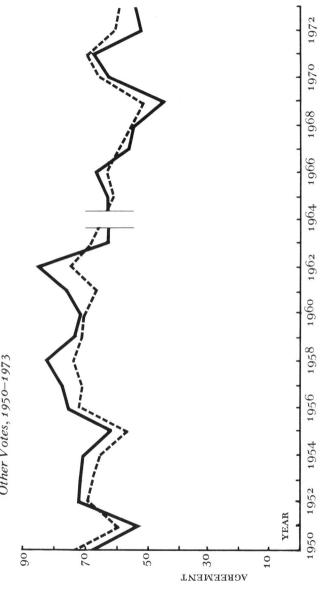

FIGURE 9. *Agreement Averages of Dependencies and Nondependencies on Other Votes, 1950–1973*

Tests of the Foreign Policy Propositions

LINEAR COMPLIANCE

The first of these propositions predicts that, for a dependent country, there is a positive linear relationship between the magnitude of its dependence and the extent of its foreign policy compliance. This very simple expectation has, of course, since been amended to apply only to issues salient to the dominant partner, and this modification will be applied to each of the analyses that follow. In application to the countries in question here, the hypothesis derived from the modified proposition is:

Hypothesis 1. The greater is its economic dependence, the greater is a dependency's agreement with the United States on Cold War roll calls.

Knowing already that dependence scores are often subject to large fluctuations, the statistical test is a bivariate regression of the form

$$IA_t = a + bD_t.$$

This equation allows a country's dependence to change in either direction, predicting only that its voting behavior will be correspondingly higher or lower. The coefficients for Cold War votes regressed on dependence appear in Table 10, along with those for Other votes as an interpretive aid.

The hypothesis states that the regression coefficient of dependence is positive, and this is borne out in seventeen of the twenty-three cases. However, the *t*-tests indicate that only seven of the positive associations are reliable estimates; many others may well have a true value of zero;[18] the same can be said of all but Liberia and the Dominican Republic among those with negative estimates. This frequent unreliability is not so surprising in view of the rather short time series available for a number of these countries. But the values of many of the coefficients are also quite small, and the spread of points around the straight line is usually great (yielding low R^2 values). Of course, the small size of the coefficients in this test and in the regressions that follow arises partly from the greater random error component in the economic measures than in the roll call data.[19] Nevertheless, should they happen to be accurate estimates despite the prevailing statistical uncertainty, there are still relatively few dependencies for which Cold War positions change dramatically as a linear function of their vulnerability to economic pressure from the United States. At most, only Nationalist China can be said to vote in direct proportion to its dependence, although there is also something of the predicted relationship for Jamaica, Cuba, and a few others even less strongly.

Finally, and particularly because there is so little support for the hypothesis, it is instructive to compare the results for Other votes on the right side of Table 8. Here, one sees that fourteen of the twenty-three regression coefficients are positive, barely fewer than for Cold War resolutions. However, this time only three are reliable as opposed to seven before, giving just minimal credence to the first hypothesis. In sum, one must search diligently to find glimmerings of support for the first hypothesis. Despite the group differences observed earlier, the higher Cold War agreement of dependencies with the U.S. would seem to be unrelated to changes in their economic status.

The linear hypothesis may nevertheless be rescued if one entertains the prospect that there may be an appreciable time lag between economic cause and political effect. In this study, it might be supposed that simultaneous annual observations of the independent and dependent variables are inappropriate. That is, governments and hence their U.N. representatives are unlikely to behave on the basis of current international economic transactions. Indeed, there may be no way to know how extensively one's

Table 10. *Coefficients for Linear Compliance*

Country	b(D)	Cold War Votes (t)	
Panama	.25	(2.83)	.2
Bolivia	.14	(.99)	.0
Liberia	− .61	(−5.06)	.8
Jamaica	.50	(2.18)	.4
China, Taiwan	.45	(3.84)	.7
Dominican Republic	− .31	(−2.88)	.3
Honduras	− .06	(− .31)	.0
Trinidad/Tobago	1.80	(1.32)	.3
Nicaragua	.06	(.17)	.0
Cuba	1.72	(1.95)	.3
Costa Rica	− .17	(− .58)	.0
Guyana	.32	(.76)	.0
Haiti	.55	(.41)	.0
El Salvador	.39	(.70)	.0
Guatemala	.25	(1.06)	.0
Indonesia	− .10	(− .70)	.0
Venezuela	.41	(2.45)	.2
Ecuador	− .11	(− .22)	.0
Paraguay	.85	(2.16)	.2
Peru	1.76	(2.67)	.2
Philippines	.12	(.29)	.0
Chile	.46	(1.45)	.1
Colombia	1.18	(1.74)	.1

economy relies on another's until after the fact, when the tallies are summed for the year. Thus, its votes in one Assembly session may more plausibly reflect the degree of a dependency's vulnerability one or two years earlier.

Accordingly, second and third operational versions of the linear hypothesis merely substitute a country's dependence score for the previous year (D_{t-1}) and the year be-

b(D)	Other Votes (t)	R²
.18	(2.60)	.243
.12	(.96)	.055
− .03	(− .24)	.011
.12	(.75)	.100
.58	(1.59)	.388
.03	(.32)	.006
− .10	(− .53)	.015
− .91	(− .90)	.167
.98	(3.06)	.369
− .76	(− .93)	.125
− .45	(−1.42)	.101
− .35	(−1.62)	.303
.97	(1.22)	.158
.57	(.98)	.088
− .17	(− .93)	.046
.22	(1.39)	.138
.25	(1.98)	.188
− .15	(− .41)	.009
.52	(1.76)	.154
.60	(1.27)	.072
− .26	(− .97)	.045
.12	(.69)	.024
.81	(1.45)	.091

fore that (D_{t-2}) for its dependence in the same year (D_t) as its voting. Hence the equations

$$IA_t = a + bD_{t-1} \text{ and } IA_t = a + bD_{t-2},$$

which are again calculated separately for the two sets of resolutions and reported in Tables 11 and 12.

Despite the plausibility of entering a lagged term into

Table 11. *Linear Compliance with One-Year Lag*

Country	Cold War Votes b(D_{t-1})	(t)	R^2	Other Votes b(D_{t-1})	(t)	R^2
Panama	.20	(2.06)	.182	.10	(1.25)	.076
Bolivia	− .01	(− .04)	.000	.33	(2.13)	.259
Liberia	−1.18	(− .58)	.078	.57	(− .62)	.086
Jamaica	.29	(.96)	.154	.04	(− .21)	.009
China, Taiwan	.18	(.84)	.258	.77	(1.88)	.638
Dominican Republic	− .34	(−3.17)	.385	.17	(−1.64)	.144
Honduras	− .17	(− .76)	.035	.02	(.11)	.001
Trinidad/Tobago	−1.77	(−2.89)	.807	.11	(.11)	.006
Nicaragua	.40	(1.22)	.096	.45	(1.17)	.089
Cuba	2.41	(4.29)	.786	.50	(.94)	.150
Costa Rica	.12	(.32)	.006	.80	(−2.27)	.244
Guyana	− .28	(− .57)	.061	.05	(− .16)	.005
Haiti	−1.10	(− .63)	.062	.56	(.51)	.042
El Salvador	.83	(1.30)	.175	.31	(.42)	.022
Guatemala	.17	(.66)	.027	.04	(.25)	.004
Indonesia	.23	(1.48)	.179	.18	(− .93)	.079
Venezuela	.31	(1.58)	.142	.41	(3.97)	.512
Ecuador	− .10	(.17)	.002	.60	(−1.53)	.128
Paraguay	1.13	(3.02)	.378	.42	(1.27)	.097
Peru	1.75	(2.46)	.242	.73	(1.52)	.109
Philippines	− .07	(− .15)	.001	.39	(1.51)	.112
Chile	.38	(1.09)	.066	.10	(− .50)	.014
Colombia	.99	(1.26)	.077	.29	(.45)	.011

Table 12. *Linear Compliance with Two-Year Lag*

Country	Cold War Votes $b(D_{t-2})$	(t)	R^2	Other Votes $b(D_{t-2})$	(t)	R^2
Panama	.11	(.97)	.047	.16	(1.88)	.158
Bolivia	.23	(2.70)	.477	.11	(.75)	.065
Liberia	.42	(.99)	.163	.11	(.51)	.050
Jamaica	−2.62	(−2.50)	.472	− .07	(− .10)	.002
China, Taiwan	.23	(3.00)	.499	.03	(.25)	.007
Dominican Republic	− .39	(−3.98)	.497	− .28	(−3.42)	.422
Honduras	− .11	(− .61)	.023	.10	(.54)	.018
Trinidad/Tobago	−1.51	(−1.05)	.136	− .21	(− .43)	.026
Nicaragua	− .61	(−2.53)	.445	− .41	(− .93)	.097
Cuba	.41	(.24)	.015	.88	(2.48)	.607
Costa Rica	− .46	(−1.32)	.098	− .27	(− .70)	.030
Guyana	.30	(.59)	.081	.57	(1.82)	.454
Haiti	−1.18	(− .59)	.019	1.24	(.73)	.029
El Salvador	− .59	(− .85)	.037	.41	(.74)	.028
Guatemala	.51	(1.41)	.110	.06	(.22)	.003
Indonesia	− .55	(−4.05)	.477	− .75	(−3.11)	.349
Venezuela	.24	(1.17)	.083	.15	(1.01)	.064
Ecuador	−1.37	(−2.69)	.311	−1.06	(−3.08)	.372
Paraguay	− .40	(− .48)	.019	.56	(.85)	.057
Peru	1.77	(−2.62)	.266	.21	(.42)	.009
Philippines	− .22	(− .48)	.013	.37	(1.30)	.086
Chile	− .18	(− .45)	.012	− .22	(−1.07)	.063
Colombia	1.43	(1.88)	.157	.37	(.56)	.016

the original equation, the outcome is even less supportive in these alternative trials. Fewer Cold War coefficients have the predicted, positive sign, and, more significantly, fewer positive associations are reliable estimates, whether the lag is for one year or two. Suppose that the necessary time delay differs among these countries. How impressive are the combined results of Tables 11 and 12? Together, they yield only seven reliably positive associations for Cold War votes. Added to the initial (unlagged) test results, just nine countries behave as predicted. Similarly, the straightline fit of the observations remains generally poor. Finally, the results of the two lagged procedures applied to Other votes hardly differ from before. In fact, in Tables 11 and 12 there is no effective difference between the predictive power of dependence for the two roll call categories. In sum, even allowing voting behavior to follow after dependence by one or two years and collapsing results produce Cold War associations barely stronger than the dubious corroboration found in the first test alone.

DECREASING MARGINAL COMPLIANCE

The fact that few countries vote with the U.S. in linear proportion to their dependence scores may be the result of forces that bring about a curvilinear pattern. It is in this fashion that the second compliance proposition differs from the first by suggesting that economic leverage exerted by a dominant country can produce only decreasing marginal political gains. National interests of dependent countries may frequently differ from those of the dominant partner, and, at some point, those differences may not be further compromised by the foreign policymakers in dependent societies. Instead, these officials may pursue their own perceived interests even though such behavior might entail some risk of economic reprisal. Of course, a country operating under conditions of relatively low dependence could satisfy the terms of its exchanges with the dominant partner by complying sufficiently often on matters of interest to the latter, while still preserving for itself other opportunities to follow its own national interests. On the other hand, if its dependence is relatively great, its divergent interests place the government in a tighter bind. In these circumstances, it may comply somewhat more than when its dependence is at a lower level, but proportionately less so.

A compatible but different explanation ascribes to the dominant country decreasing marginal utility to its dependencies' compliance, even on issues that it finds salient. Either or both of these rationales lead to the following hypothesis:

Hypothesis 2. Greater economic dependence yields decreasingly more frequent agreement with the United States on Cold War roll calls.

This prediction can be translated into a linear equation stating that

$$\ln(\Delta IA_t) = \ln(a) + b(\ln D_{t\text{-}1}),$$

where ln = natural logarithms of the terms;

ΔIA_t = the change in a dependency's voting agreement with the U.S. from year $t-1$ to year t;

$D_{t\text{-}1}$ = a dependency's dependence score for year $t-1$.

Following common practice with logarithmic functions, the equation for each country is originally formulated in a nonlinear, multiplicative fashion.[20] It is then transformed, using logarithms to represent rates of change, and the coefficients are estimated using an ordinary-least-squares procedure. The use of "natural" logarithms is a technique that allows each country's observations to best fit a smooth curve that may differ in two ways from the curves of other countries. Two differences among dependencies may occur. One difference may be the initial intercept, reflecting a country's relative level of voting agreement. The other is the percentage rate at which that country's voting agreement changes with a 1 percent change in levels of dependence (the elasticity of voting agreement with respect to dependence), reflecting its particular tendency to display decreasing marginal compliance. The first of these estimates, for the intercept, is thus a control variable in the sense that the dependencies agree with the United States at different average levels. Therefore, the third and fourth columns bear the greatest theoretical import among the results listed in Table 13.

The hypothesis predicts reliably positive coefficients for dependence in the third and fourth columns. However, among the entire population there are only four reliable estimates, and three of them are negative! Thus, only Liberia displays decreasing marginal compliance on Cold War votes. But this outcome might properly be regarded with suspicion. The law of large numbers says that among twenty-three trials there is a high probability that by chance alone occasional cases will conform to expectations. On this basis, it is tempting to dismiss the Liberian coefficient as a random result.

There is, on the other hand, clear evidence in the preceding chapter that the U.S. dependencies are not homogeneous. Accordingly, the law of large numbers may properly be rejected in favor of efforts to seek out those other Liberian attributes that would plausibly explain its unique position in Table 13. In advance of such a task, however, it is more efficient to entertain another rival hypothesis based on what is already known about the Liberian data: the time-series indicators of its economic dependence on the United States are unavoidably short, spanning just the last nine years of the period.[21] With a lagged term in the equation, the coefficient is based on just eight observations and is therefore quite susceptible to bias introduced by statistical outliers.[22]

Table 13. *Coefficients for Decreasing Marginal Cold War Compliance*

Country	ln(a)	(t)	b(lnD$_{t-1}$)	(t)	R^2
Panama	1.80	(.91)	− .24	(− .52)	.014
Bolivia	5.90	(2.28)	− 1.36	(−2.06)	.247
Liberia	−9.82	(−3.36)	2.92	(3.56)	.679
Jamaica	− .96	(− .50)	.40	(.78)	.110
China, Taiwan	5.72	(2.95)	− 1.55	(−2.64)	.778
Dominican Republic	1.14	(1.51)	− .06	(− .26)	.004
Honduras	2.03	(2.16)	− .31	(−1.03)	.062
Trinidad/Tobago	38.88	(9.42)	−11.55	(−9.04)	.976
Nicaragua	−2.76	(− .81)	1.04	(1.04)	.118
Cuba	.41	(.04)	.35	(.12)	.003
Costa Rica	−4.41	(−1.31)	1.68	(1.59)	.136
Guyana	1.30	(.32)	− .20	(− .16)	.005
Haiti	8.40	(1.55)	− 2.73	(−1.39)	.244
El Salvador	− .22	(− .07)	.49	(.44)	.023
Guatemala	2.05	(2.15)	− .40	(−1.28)	.094
Indonesia	− .63	(− .60)	.51	(1.48)	.180
Venezuela	.93	(1.48)	− .14	(− .19)	.002
Ecuador	.48	(.16)	.26	(.24)	.004
Paraguay	.31	(.43)	.26	(.93)	.054
Peru	.27	(.22)	.06	(.14)	.001
Philippines	1.92	(2.03)	− .44	(−1.22)	.076
Chile	.66	(1.17)	.14	(.70)	.028
Colombia	− .38	(− .17)	.43	(.54)	.015

Figure 10 shows that one outlier is indeed responsible for the misleading coefficient for Liberia. As annual changes in voting agreement are plotted against dependence, there is a shapeless cluster owing to relatively little variance in the economic measure. Thus, the single outlier representing one year's very high dependence followed in the next Assembly session by a large upward voting change allows the logged regression coefficient to approximate the curve drawn here. In short, the Liberian anomaly is apparently a statistical artifact rather than a substantive exception to the rejection of the decreasing marginal compliance hypothesis.

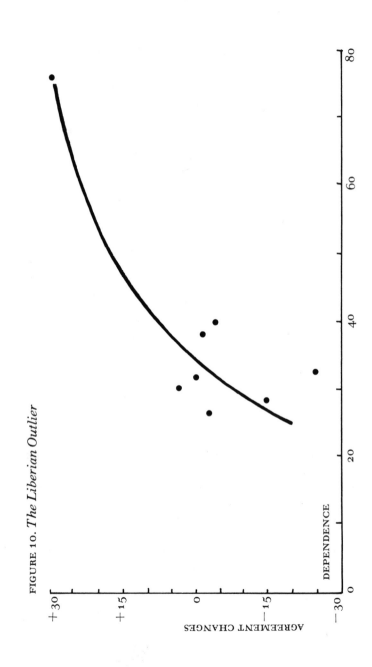

FIGURE 10. *The Liberian Outlier*

DEFIANCE

If compliance is never logarithmic with respect to dependence, and is convincingly linear in only three cases, the third competing proposition offers another curvilinear possibility. This remaining static expectation is based on the idea that dominance breeds resentment. Resentment itself is meant to denote a sense of injustice perceived by influential members of the dependent society and aimed at the dominant partner. Such a reaction may mean that a dependency's foreign policy behavior will be defiant rather than compliant. Two assumptions have been introduced in order to specify this possibility. First, it was posited that resentment increases in linear proportion to the extent of dependence. Second, it has been assumed that the propensity to defy covaries directly with resentment: the greater the resentment, the more frequent will be the inclination to defy. Thus, defiance propensities become a linear function of dependence. This, of course, represents a force directly countervailing that of linear compliance. When the two are combined, foreign policy compliance is proposed to follow a parabolic curve.

The resultant hypothesis is:

Hypothesis 3. A dependency's Cold War voting agreement with the U.S. is lowest when its dependence is either lowest or greatest; maximum agreement occurs at intermediate levels of dependence.

Reference in this hypothesis to intermediate dependence is, of course, relative to the range experienced by each particular country. In other words, it is explicitly proposed that these countries' differing ranges of dependence are unimportant to their foreign policy behavior. What is said to matter is the extent of a country's dependence in any one year relative to its dependence level in other years. Thus, not only may a dependence score of, say, 20 usually have greater impact in one country than in another, but that score may also represent abnormally high penetration for the first yet not for the second.[23] Especially because the hypothesis rests so heavily on psychological ground, it seems wise to regard each dependence score as relative to a country-specific norm.

The hypothesis is tested by examining each country's scatterplot, where each specific point is a coordinate of Cold War agreement and dependence for a given year. More elaborate tests could be undertaken,[24] but this simpler procedure is suggested by two considerations. First, statistics can be seriously affected by outliers when there exist rather few observations. This has already proved to be a problem in the instance of Liberia, and its potential extends to several other dependencies. Second, it is difficult for most readers to visualize statistical definitions of complex curves without ultimately resorting to graphic displays.

It is, of course, very unlikely that the scatterplots for China (Taiwan), Jamaica, or Cuba would indicate a parabolic relationship here, since the same two variables earlier yielded linear regression coefficients for these three countries. This is, indeed, the case. Among the remaining twenty dependencies, the actual distribution resembles the hypothesized curve in only three cases, as illustrated with Peruvian data in Figure 11.

One interesting feature of the test's generally unsupportive results concerns the role of U.S. private investment. Because motives to defy have been attributed to resentment, there was some a priori basis for suspecting that the hypothesis would describe particularly well the foreign policy behavior of those dependencies that are especially reliant on private investment. It is the multinational corporation that has been called a lightning rod for the antagonism toward foreign domination in dependent societies. Among the three modes of economic penetration, foreign investment is the dominant contributor to Panamanian and Jamaican dependence; for the others, investment is no

more than equal to trade and/or aid flows (see Chapter 4, Table 4). However, the countries that conform to the defiance hypothesis are Peru, Trinidad and Tobago, and Guyana,[25] and decidedly not Panama or Jamaica. Thus, as a mediating factor, dependence on investment flows relative to trade and aid resources does not successfully discriminate between the three countries with parabolic curves and the remaining twenty with other configurations. (This question, in particular, could more appropriately be addressed with an accumulated investment ratio.)

A closely related theoretical lead points to investments in primary goods production as particularly apt to trigger resentment owing to their greater visibility and symbolic representation of exploitation. Unfortunately, investment data disaggregated into figures specific to types of production are even less often made available than are national aggregates. However, some rough idea of investment book values in different economic sectors offers a first approximation for certain countries of interest here.

In the cases of Panama and Jamaica, where investment flows are high relative to trade and aid, the 1973 book values indicate an important difference.[26] Accumulated U.S. investments in Panama are considerably diversified, and are no more than about 20 percent concentrated in unprocessed goods. Thus, emphasizing the negative political repercussions of primary goods investment would not suggest Panama as a promising candidate for defiant foreign policy behavior. In Jamaica, on the other hand, perhaps as much as half of the U.S. ownership is in mining and smelting of bauxite ore. One would therefore expect Jamaican Cold War agreement with the United States to follow the hypothesized parabolic curve. Quite to the contrary, Jamaican Cold War voting is more closely a linear function of its total dependence.

What, then, of the distribution of private investment in those three countries where dependence (via resentment) appears to affect foreign policy as predicted? The first thing to be said is that the pertinent data are simply not available for either Trinidad and Tobago or Guyana. In the case of Peru, however, the 1973 book value of U.S. investments supports the notion that foreign-owned primary goods industries have distinctive political implications. More than one-half of U.S. investment there is concentrated in mining and smelting operations. Furthermore, when petroleum interests are added, the total share rises to over 70 percent of all U.S. investments.[27] Peru is only one case, however, and the implications should not be overdrawn. Indeed, the illustrations here, including both Peru and the contradictory evidence regarding Jamaica, by no means represent a patterned relationship between the sectoral distribution of foreign investment within a dependent country and the foreign policy consequences of that penetration. More adequate economic data might resolve the issue, but for now it must remain an open question.

What is left is the fact that just three dependencies exhibit foreign policy behavior consistent with the defiance proposition. Add to that group the three other countries for which there is a positive and linear association between compliance and dependence, and the broader impression is that economic vulnerabilities are not systematically reflected in the international politics of the General Assembly. Such a conclusion, however, is premature for reasons that will shortly become clear. Therefore, the term "compliance" continues to be invoked despite its seeming incongruity with the weight of the static analyses just described.

DETERIORATING COMPLIANCE

Recall that the fourth proposition is explicitly dynamic, asserting that a dependency's foreign policy compliance deteriorates over time. The plausible justifications are several, including a dominant country's control difficulties when faced with the proliferation of sovereign dependencies, the political pressures applied to a dependent state by an awakening, newly mobilized populace, the eventual politicization of resentment fostered by dependence, and the growing international solidarity among poor countries of the world. By any or all of these processes, the behavioral proposition is that compliance should decline.

Such facilitative conditions as just enumerated have perhaps never emerged more simultaneously and forcefully than among poor countries in the last three decades. Thus, the evidence marshaled here should be especially well suited to a test of the following hypothesis:

> *Hypothesis 4.* A dependency's Cold War voting agreement with the United States decreases over time.

Considering the evidence documenting an average decline for the group's voting agreement, one might suppose that this study has already uncovered deteriorating compliance. This is not necessarily the case, however. The group decline may owe to factors other than those in question here. For example, group dependence averages also decline after the early 1960s, and dependence was earlier seen to share statistical association with Cold War voting for several group members. One must also take into account voting declines for nondependent countries if changing dominant-dependent relations are to be distinguished from *global* patterns of Assembly voting agreement with the United States. This reasoning produces a procedure that sorts out the effects of "time" from the two sources of interference just mentioned: changing levels of dependence and shifts in the roll call behavior of nondependent states. The multivariate equation for the test can be represented as

$$IA_t = a + b_1 D_t + b_2 \overline{IA}_t + b_3 t,$$

where $\overline{IA}_t$ = mean Cold War voting agreement with the U.S. for non-dependencies;

t = time (1950, 1951, 1952, . . . 1973)

Before considering the statistical results of this test reported in Table 14, one should recall that the underlying proposition is not guided by a particular linear or curvilinear expectation. Declines in compliance attributable to the types of forces under consideration here may well be uneven across time. The prediction is merely that compliance will decline. Thus, the scatter reflected in R^2 values is not of much immediate theoretical interest. Similarly, the magnitude of the regression coefficient for "time" is rather less consequential than the search for negative coefficients.

Contrary to expectations, there is virtually no indication that agreement with the U.S. on Cold War votes deteriorates as an independent function of time.[28] Fewer than half of the regression coefficients for time take a negative sign, and only two of them (Liberia and Guyana) are reliable. Moreover, among the positive coefficients, only two or three more are reliable (Nationalist China, Cuba, and Guatemala). In short, time has no systematic effect in either direction on the voting behavior of dependencies independent of the control variables; corroboration of the deterioration hypothesis simply does not materialize. Under these circumstances, the results for the other two independent (control) variables become especially intriguing.

First, notice that entering dependence into this linear regression equation has the effect of retesting the first proposition more elaborately than before. That is, the partial regression coefficients for dependence have a substantive import identical to the bivariate estimates seen earlier. In this larger equation, however, the potential effects represented by the two remaining independent variables are separated from dependence itself. Is dependence more substantially related to Cold War voting behavior this time? Compared to the bivariate results in Table 8, the current results differ in one sense rather little: the coefficients' signs change in only three cases, and none of them is reliable. More telling, however, is that only two positive and

Table 14. *Coefficients for Deteriorating Compliance on Cold War Votes*

Country	b(D)	(t)
Panama	.04	(.59
Bolivia	.12	(.81
Liberia	− .76	(−3.54
Jamaica	− .26	(− .90
China, Taiwan	.77	(3.00
Dominican Republic	− .14	(−1.06
Honduras	− .05	(− .32
Trinidad/Tobago	5.44	(1.51
Nicaragua	.06	(.28
Cuba	.12	(.11
Costa Rica	− .16	(− .51
Guyana	.23	(1.14
Haiti	1.64	(1.30
El Salvador	.61	(1.14
Guatemala	.03	(.12
Indonesia	− .05	(− .36
Venezuela	.11	(.64
Ecuador	.56	(1.09
Paraguay	.44	(.94
Peru	1.06	(2.08
Philippines	− .44	(−1.43
Chile	.44	(1.67
Colombia	.25	(.36

reliable associations (Nationalist China and Peru) appear when the controls are introduced, whereas earlier there were seven such cases. Finally, of the three best fits earlier —Nationalist China, Jamaica, and Cuba—only the first survives the introduction of control variables. This means that the limited support for the first compliance hypothesis has now virtually evaporated altogether.

What remains from this test is the considerable rela-

b(t)	(t)	b($\overline{IA}$)	(t)	R^2
.09	(.17)	1.32	(3.61)	.723
1.35	(1.61)	1.02	(1.54)	.214
−3.13	(−2.54)	.86	(1.45)	.917
−2.89	(−1.64)	2.37	(2.34)	.885
2.69	(2.28)	.37	(1.51)	.950
− .63	(− .86)	.45	(.77)	.455
.66	(.95)	1.22	(2.46)	.351
−8.24	(−1.10)	− .70	(− .38)	.656
−1.31	(−1.19)	.52	(.93)	.621
3.64	(2.06)	.52	(.86)	.718
.51	(.81)	.58	(1.31)	.119
−5.53	(−4.08)	− .22	(− .41)	.867
−2.35	(−1.18)	.68	(.80)	.484
1.49	(.74)	1.63	(1.56)	.330
2.00	(1.85)	1.10	(1.54)	.225
1.55	(1.68)	.91	(1.82)	.278
−1.34	(−1.47)	.37	(.61)	.544
.22	(.23)	1.44	(2.21)	.346
.69	(.75)	1.04	(2.00)	.419
− .45	(− .53)	1.32	(.21)	.717
1.00	(1.47)	2.02	(4.71)	.661
.41	(.45)	1.63	(2.45)	.481
− .87	(−1.12)	.50	(.83)	.456

tionship between the Cold War voting of dependencies and other countries. All but two coefficients are positive, eight of them reliably so. These statistical results are not overpoweringly strong, of course. But they do stand very much in contrast to those for the two other predictors of voting behavior. Thus, the emergent impression from this multivariate test is that neither time nor decreasing dependence accounts for the waning propensity of dependencies to agree with the U.S. on Cold War resolutions. Instead, it seems that the deterioration more closely follows a pattern common to all Assembly delegates.

If dependencies are in fact responsive only to voting pressures common to all U.N. voters, as just suggested, then a parallel test of the three independent variables should yield the same outcome when their effects on Other roll calls are scrutinized. That is, issue salience should not be a relevant distinction if the United States does not exert economic leverage on the dependent states. Accordingly, Table 15 reports the same multiple regression estimating procedure applied to Other votes.

The partial coefficients for all three variables bear a strong resemblance to their counterparts for Cold War issues. For example, there are again sixteen positive estimates for the dependence predictor, and very few of them are reliable. Also, the relationship between "time" and agreement with the U.S. is again mixed, with a modestly stronger tendency to assume the predicted negative association in this second trial; the pattern remains unconvincing. However, the coefficients for agreement with nondependent countries are especially noteworthy here. On roll calls of low salience to the U.S., its dependencies' votes with and against the dominant state very much coincide with the changing average among the remainder of the Assembly membership. Indeed, the only possible exceptions to this impressive pattern are three positive coefficients whose unreliability may be casualties of rather short time series. Thus, it is now clear that the earlier group averages for Other issues did not conceal notably deviant dependencies.

The results of this fourth hypothesis bear larger implications as well. As a multivariate test, the equation has not only retested the first hypothesis with greater validity, it has entered two factors that were previously untested, time and Assembly voting changes common to the entirety of the U.N. membership. In conjunction with results of the

Table 15. *Coefficients for Deteriorating Compliance on Other Votes*

Country	b(D)	(t)	b(t)	(t)	b(IA)	(t)	R²
Panama	.01	(.07)	−.13	(− .41)	1.48	(3.44)	.549
Bolivia	−.00	(− .06)	−.37	(−1.25)	1.45	(4.67)	.701
Liberia	−2.26	(− .18)	1.25	(1.74)	1.03	(2.87)	.681
Jamaica	−.00	(− .00)	−1.36	(−1.51)	1.42	(4.58)	.888
China, Taiwan	.71	(.38)	1.59	(.15)	1.22	(.53)	.499
Dominican Republic	.23	(2.25)	−.99	(−2.15)	.95	(2.23)	.450
Honduras	−.14	(− .92)	.19	(.40)	1.36	(2.82)	.358
Trinidad/Tobago	1.25	(.89)	−4.50	(−1.12)	.20	(.17)	.671
Nicaragua	.62	(2.44)	−.07	(.06)	1.46	(1.82)	.660
Cuba	−1.83	(−2.78)	2.66	(1.91)	.67	(1.79)	.793
Costa Rica	.16	(.75)	.16	(.59)	1.70	(5.69)	.712
Guyana	.00	(.00)	.31	(.41)	1.45	(3.48)	.829
Haiti	.57	(1.00)	.87	(1.19)	1.54	(3.74)	.748
El Salvador	.67	(2.57)	−1.26	(−1.26)	1.54	(2.59)	.854
Guatemala	.17	(1.10)	−.20	(.52)	1.75	(4.26)	.548
Indonesia	.18	(2.46)	−.54	(−1.67)	.86	(3.43)	.859
Venezuela	.09	(1.02)	−.61	(−1.75)	1.21	(4.12)	.755
Ecuador	.18	(.94)	−.53	(−1.88)	1.65	(6.83)	.824
Paraguay	.04	(.13)	−.65	(−1.60)	.86	(2.72)	.607
Peru	.24	(.69)	.10	(.27)	1.92	(5.15)	.641
Philippines	−.68	(3.64)	−1.11	(−3.88)	.79	(2.90)	.732
Chile	−.05	(− .43)	−.18	(− .76)	1.38	(5.23)	.672
Colombia	.16	(.38)	.23	(.72)	1.84	(4.83)	.604

second and third (curvilinear) hypotheses, the outcome of the fourth hypothesis brings the discussion back to the postponed question, "Are dependencies compliant in their foreign policy behavior?" The weight of the evidence now suggests that "compliance" is a misnomer in application to foreign policy activity in the General Assembly. Rather than compliance, what seems to happen is that dependencies are responsive to forces that act similarly on all delegations to the U.N. However, it is advisable not to drop the matter here. Two brief forays back into the voting data can provide alternative views of the foreign policy behavior of the dependencies. In so doing, these analyses can further probe the tentative appraisals that have emerged, namely, that dependencies are not compliant and that their voting parallels the behavior of other countries.

Tests of Alternative Explanations

INCREMENTALISM

There is a wide range of potential explanations of foreign policy behavior. Whereas economic dependence is one plausible set of external determinants of policy, a competing approach emphasizes internal bureaucratic politics that may shape a government's foreign policy behavior. This alternative perspective draws attention to competition among self-interested, parochial participants. The immediate result of this bureaucratic competition is compromise, and the emergent pattern from a series of compromises is one of very slow, incremental change. The important difference between compliance motivated by dependence and incremental foreign policy behavior is that the former is cast as part of a purposeful exchange while the latter is not. This difference implies that compliance is subject to rapid changes as dependencies adapt to their environment, whereas incremental foreign policymaking is at best only sluggishly responsive to external conditions.

The question at hand is, of course, whether the dependencies of the United States follow an incremental course in their Assembly voting over a period of years. This question is made all the more interesting by the discovery that dependence itself is such a poor voting predictor. A first impression of the dependencies' incrementalist propensities can be obtained by regressing the scores of their annual voting agreement with the U.S. in adjacent years, following the formula

$$IA_t = a + b_1 IA_{t-1} + b_2 D_t.$$

The second factor, dependence, is entered into the equation in order to better estimate the repetition reflected in the first coefficient. Applying this equation to the two sets of roll calls generates findings detailed in Tables 16 and 17.

Led by Guyana, the Philippines, and Peru, there are numerous dependencies for which agreement with U.S. Cold War positions changes only slowly over time. Given the greater diversity of substantive matters in the residual category of Other votes, and thus greater annual changes in the content of those votes, it comes as no surprise to discover that there is less evidence of incrementalism in the second of these tables.[29] Meanwhile, dependence scores again fail to assume linear relationships with voting on either set of Assembly resolutions.

In short, the incrementalism approach highlights a considerable strain of voting repetition among the dependencies on Cold War issues and simultaneously confirms once again the relative impotence of the economic dependence factor. On the other hand, voting repetition can occur for reasons other than bureaucratic politics. The stability of the U.N. agenda over time, for example, may account for voting stability.

Neither of these possibilities can explain, however, the one seemingly anomalous result of the analyses in this chapter: if changing dependence is not systematically re-

Table 16. *Serial Regression Coefficients for Cold War Votes*

Country	IA$_{t-1}$	(t)	D$_t$	(t)	R^2
Panama	.68	(2.20)	.15	(1.24)	.466
Bolivia	.36	(1.37)	.14	(1.31)	.385
Liberia	− .09	(− .14)	−1.41	(−1.63)	.474
Jamaica	.02	(3.55)	.12	(.05)	.001
China, Taiwan	.58	(4.74)	.14	(1.88)	.739
Dominican Republic	.47	(2.51)	− .32	(−2.72)	.587
Honduras	.56	(2.43)	− .03	(− .17)	.285
Trinidad/Tobago	.30	(.93)	−2.22	(−2.99)	.693
Nicaragua	.52	(1.35)	.35	(1.08)	.242
Cuba	.14	(.37)	1.82	(2.00)	.636
Costa Rica	− .07	(− .24)	− .19	(− .57)	.022
Guyana	.89	(2.21)	.38	(1.17)	.603
Haiti	.56	(1.97)	1.80	(.85)	.219
El Salvador	.53	(2.26)	− .05	(− .08)	.235
Guatemala	.49	(2.35)	.31	(1.49)	.324
Indonesia	.17	(.94)	− .14	(−1.23)	.147
Venezuela	.58	(3.08)	.35	(2.49)	.569
Ecuador	.21	(.80)	.09	(.17)	.041
Paraguay	.35	(1.27)	.60	(.71)	.155
Peru	.95	(7.90)	.38	(1.01)	.841
Philippines	.85	(4.59)	.14	(.34)	.561
Chile	.74	(3.19)	.22	(.80)	.454
Colombia	.62	(2.66)	.50	(.71)	.379

lated to shifts in the Cold War voting behavior of these countries, and if changes in their agreement levels parallel those of nondependent states, then why is the average agreement with the U.S. of these twenty-three dependencies so much higher than the average for the remaining members of the U.N.?

REGIONALISM

This question may usefully be addressed by adopting a regional view of international politics. Regionalism holds out at least momentary hope for an answer to the question of different group voting averages since nineteen of the twenty-three dependencies are located in Latin America. Recall that a regional focus fosters the belief that geographic clusters of nations have similar and distinctive foreign policies. Applied to the concerns of this study, such a proposition implies that the nineteen Latin dependencies should vote on Cold War issues differently from Liberia, China, Indonesia, and the Philippines. This expectation is confirmed by averaging the annual agreement scores within these two subsets of dependent countries. Those in the western hemisphere agree with the U.S. position 68.5 percent of the time, whereas the four nonwestern dependencies register just 56 percent agreement. In fact, the four dependencies outside the region agree with the U.S. at virtually the

Table 17. *Serial Regression Coefficients for Other Votes*

Country	IA_{t-1}	(t)	D_t	(t)	R^2
Panama	.15	(.75)	.24	(2.92)	.456
Bolivia	.52	(1.06)	— .02	(— .06)	.235
Liberia	.41	(1.02)	— .41	(—1.16)	.266
Jamaica	— .09	(— .20)	.40	(.34)	.028
China, Taiwan	.21	(.70)	— .13	(—1.37)	.269
Dominican Republic	.48	(2.04)	.03	(.02)	.218
Honduras	.18	(.80)	— .13	(— .79)	.058
Trinidad/Tobago	— .08	(— .25)	— .66	(—2.11)	.492
Nicaragua	.44	(1.36)	.55	(1.52)	.360
Cuba	— .22	(— .90)	— .41	(— .80)	.276
Costa Rica	.13	(.53)	— .47	(—1.39)	.120
Guyana	.20	(.48)	— .36	(—1.38)	.335
Haiti	.28	(1.23)	2.12	(1.14)	.202
El Salvador	55	(2.71)	— .06	(— .12)	.290
Guatemala	— .06	(— .24)	— .17	(— .92)	.056
Indonesia	.26	(1.99)	.05	(.38)	.192
Venezuela	.44	(1.87)	.21	(1.67)	.357
Ecuador	.47	(2.08)	.04	(.11)	.223
Paraguay	.52	(2.07)	.57	(.95)	.391
Peru	.46	(2.20)	.28	(.62)	.272
Philippines	.45	(2.11)	— .01	(— .04)	.207
Chile	.31	(1.24)	.05	(.25)	.113
Colombia	.24	(1.03)	.70	(1.12)	.149

same average level as do *non*dependent states generally. It is the predominance of Latin American representation in the dependent population that pulls the group average upward.

Finally, do dependent and nondependent Latin countries vote alike? The regional perspective implies that they should. Compared to the 68.5 percent Cold War agreement of the nineteen Latin dependencies, their nondependent neighbors support the U.S. slightly less, averaging a 62.2 percent level. However, this difference should be treated with some circumspection since only five nations in the region comprise the nondependent group.[30] With this caveat in mind, it nevertheless appears that nondependent countries in the western hemisphere agree with U.S. Cold War preferences to a greater degree (62.2%) than do dependencies on other continents (56%).

To conclude that regionalism is the dominant voting influence among the factors considered in this inquiry is, of course, to beg the question. What do Latin American countries have in common that might explain their distinct voting behavior? Widespread poverty despite 150 years of self-governance? Hispanic culture? Several possibilities exist. It may strike some as odd, but it is still possible to argue that economic ties to the United States are a real possibility in this context. After all, the five "nondependent" members of the region (Barbados, Mexico, Brazil, Argentina, and Uruguay, with Cuba excepted) not only vote with the U.S. more often than do most U.N. members, they also have stronger bonds to the U.S. economy than do the great majority of the world's countries.

For this thesis to be at all persuasive, however, some explanation for the lower Cold War agreement of nonwestern dependencies must be presented. Perhaps Kenneth Boulding's "loss-of-strength gradient" idea is applicable here.[31] By this, he means that a country's ability to influence the behavior of others is diminished by distance. Accordingly, the U.S. is less able to generate voting agreement by dependent but distant Liberia, Nationalist China, Indonesia, and the Philippines than it is among nearby countries that do not meet the international dependence threshold used here. Of course, whether these ideas in combination are an accurate reflection of reality is clearly beyond the scope of this study. But they are suggestive regarding how apparent impasses are sometimes mounted.

Summary

The empirical analyses of foreign policy compliance deserve a restatement, if only because they refute the guiding theoretical propositions of this study. Except as noted, the following remarks apply only to results regarding the Cold War roll calls that have been assumed to be especially salient to the United States.

1. *Agreement with the U.S. position is not a positive function of the extent of a country's dependence.* This is true for both the linear and decreasing marginal compliance hypotheses. China (Taiwan) is perhaps the single exception, showing a strong linear association even in the presence of control variables.

2. *Agreement with the U.S. is seldom a parabolic function of the extent of a country's dependence.* Only Peru, Trinidad and Tobago, and Guyana conform to the third hypothesis. In this context, illustrative evidence suggests that neither investment dependence nor, more narrowly, dependence on investments in unprocessed goods plays a pronounced role as an agent of resentment that is translated into defiant foreign policy behavior.

3. *The dependencies' waning agreement with the U.S. is associated with a parallel decline for the whole of the General Assembly.* When this average for all U.N. members is

considered, there is scant evidence of dependence-related changes at work to bring about deteriorating agreement among the twenty-three affected countries.

4. *There is considerable repetition in the year-to-year voting behavior of many dependencies.* This is suggestive of either incrementalism or of a rather stable schedule of Assembly resolutions in view of fluctuating dependence scores that remain unrelated to U.N. voting.

5. *The fact that dependencies agree with the U.S. significantly more than do other countries may be attributable to the fact that the large majority of the dependent countries are Latin American, rather than to their dependent condition itself.* All Latin American countries agree with the U.S. at a higher level than the world average. In fact, nondependent countries in this region agree with the U.S. more often than do the four dependencies outside the western hemisphere.

These several summary statements provoke some very interesting questions. In view of these findings and those from the economic analyses in the preceding chapter, it might be surmised that the theoretical bases of the dependence or interdependence concepts have been seriously eroded. Further, one could infer from the outcome of the compliance hypotheses that economic relations between the United States and its dependencies are not important to the foreign policy decisions of either. It would be a mistake, of course, to agree to either of these generalizations without considering them at greater length. These concerns are therefore central to the concluding chapter.

among the main concerns of *dependencia* scholarship. This study has attempted to test these confluent ideas for one set of countries over a span of two dozen years. The fact that U.S. dependencies and other Latin American countries tended to agree with the U.S. in the General Assembly markedly more often than did other countries until the 1970s may be an indication that asymmetrical economic ties produced some foreign policy gains. However, more specific propositions linking annual economic changes to yearly voting shifts must be rejected on the basis of the evidence.

What theoretical implications can be drawn from these results? More specifically, why might the U.S. fail to extract compliance from its economic dependencies, especially in the last years of the study period? Keohane and Nye believe that assessments of asymmetrical interdependence provide "a first approximation" of influence opportunities available to the actors.[1] But they then suggest two types of factors that may intervene between asymmetries and successful influence: political bargaining and regime change.[2] They point out that "political bargaining is the usual means of translating potential into effects, and a lot is often lost in the translation."[3] Thus, the United States may have great influence potential emanating from its economically dominant position vis-à-vis the dependent countries, but it may nevertheless experience difficulties in its efforts to extract political concessions as political economy "payments."

The bargaining position of a country such as the United States is probably weakened by domestic fragmentation and problems of coordination within the government.[4] Consistent political pressure on other countries cannot effectively be mounted by a government that tries to balance the competing demands of diverse domestic constituents and that, in addition, is plagued by overlapping and parochially self-interested bureaucracies. At the same time, these very difficulties are not likely to be so pronounced for weak states. A dependent state may therefore have greater political resolve (or at least its appearance) than does the dominant economic partner when their foreign policy preferences conflict.

In short, the absence of a patterned relationship between changing economic dependence and General Assembly agreement with the U.S. may reflect Washington's inability to consistently translate economic opportunity into superior bargaining strength. But why should respective bargaining strengths change, as is suggested by the shift in voting patterns of the late 1960s? The answer may be that there has been a change in regime within which such bargaining takes place.

"Regime" refers to sets of rules and procedural norms that regularize the behavior of actors. The regime that governs a particular type of international relationship will partially determine, say Keohane and Nye, both the participants and the capabilities relevant to bargaining over the issues at stake in the relationship. For example, capitalist foreign trade in the aftermath of World War II developed within a regime institutionalized in 1947 as the General Agreement on Tariffs and Trade (GATT). The GATT operates with a formal code of behavior and, through bilateral and multilateral negotiations among governmental representatives, has overseen great reductions in tariffs and other artificial barriers to free trade, successfully stimulating greater trade flows among capitalist economies.

The GATT regime has more recently been challenged by poor countries. Their offensive crystallized in the formation of the United Nations Conference on Trade and Development (UNCTAD) in 1964. UNCTAD has sought to redress the perceived inequities of the terms of trade for raw materials. Their proposals are for new rules to guarantee them stable or even greater returns for their exports. In other words, UNCTAD members have been attempting to change the prevailing regime in trade relations between industrial and nonindustrial economies. In so doing, they have brought in the United Nations as a new participant, and they have seized upon the General Assembly's one-country, one-vote procedure as a mechanism for increasing their collective capability.

The emergence of a new international trade regime would not, by itself, provide a theoretical explanation for the rejection of the foreign policy hypotheses in this study. However, regime change may be associated with greater complexity in "issue structure" that precludes the application of one type of capability advantage to contests in a different issue domain.[5] It might therefore be reasoned that since at least the mid-1960s U.S. dependencies have been actively pursuing regime change through an international organization that enhances their own political capabilities. Simultaneously, the new regime splits apart U.S. economic preponderance from Washington's cold war preoccupations by denying the particular linkage between issues (and thus capabilities) that the U.S. has traditionally made.[6]

Such a division in issue structure between the "high politics" of the cold war and the "low politics" of rich-poor economics is consistent with much of the evidence seen in Chapter 5.[7] Not only were the economically motivated hypotheses rejected, but the group voting comparison between dependencies and nondependencies on Cold War issues showed that the predicted difference between them declined appreciably after the mid-1960s. Moreover, as regimes change and additional actors and cross-pressures come into play, the possible breakdown of linkages between issues invites a brief reconsideration of linkages of another sort.

Turning from the interdependence perspective to *dependencia* draws attention to the logic of foreign policy compliance as a reflection of the interlocking motives of elites in dominant and dependent societies. The existence of these transnational elite alliances is a dominant theme in *dependencia* writings, and it suggests a coherence to

elite behavior that links transnational interests and domestic behavior, including the expression of local elite
preferences in a dependency's foreign policy positions. The
existence of such transnational alliances and domestic linkages is based on impressionistic accounts, however, and
some case study evidence contradicts this portrayal.[8] In
other words, it may be that local business elites who are
tied into the foreign trade and foreign capital sectors of
their dependent economy nevertheless preserve a national
political identity. Or, if not, they may fail to be very persuasive influencers of foreign policy behavior. Thus, if
either the international issue linkage or the transnational
and domestic pressure linkage is not in fact consistently
realized, its absence would account for the unexpected results discovered for the principal foreign policy hypotheses here.

The three theoretical possibilities just reviewed—political bargaining difficulties, issue separation accompanying
regime change, and the absence of coherent transnational
and domestic linkages—are candidate explanations for the
rejection of the compliance hypotheses. Of the three, the
idea of issue separation is perhaps the most appealing because it also corresponds to known historical events, including the UNCTAD-led challenge to the GATT trade
regime and the decline thereafter in dependency support
for U.S. Cold War voting preferences in the Assembly.
However, if more were known about specific political influence attempts, the viability of one or both of the other
two possibilities might similarly be enhanced. In short,
these explanations constitute theoretical overidentification
of the empirical results.

Complicating matters further is yet another prospect:
the measurement procedures used in this study may in certain respects be significantly flawed. For example, it can
be argued that decision-makers in Washington are no longer much interested in General Assembly voting behavior
in New York. If true, then it follows that neither would

the U.S. put economic pressure on other delegates nor would representatives of dependent countries regard their votes as opportunities to make political payments of value to the dominant country. Therefore, the extent of voting agreement between dependencies and the U.S. should decline. This prediction is, of course, supported by the grouped data in the preceding chapter, where in particular the Cold War agreement levels decline after 1966. This doubt of the U.N.'s continuing importance to the U.S. does not itself rule out the possibility that compliance has successfully been extracted in the Assembly, of course. Indeed, the fact that dependencies exhibit such high levels of agreement for so many years before the decline begins may be taken, in this context, as evidence of their compliance when it was still being sought by the U.S. The inference is therefore that, if the U.S. no longer cares very much about the U.N., one should look elsewhere for behavioral data covering more recent years.

Turning to the economic measures, one finds stronger doubts about some validity properties of the indicators. Some weaknesses of these measures have been raised earlier, but one of them in particular might usefully be repeated before turning to the most intriguing possibility in this category. Regression equations have served as a primary statistical procedure in the empirical portion of this research. The resultant coefficients estimating the strength of association between independent and dependent variables necessarily reflect the distribution of measurement error in those variables. Because tests of the guiding compliance hypotheses relied almost entirely on regression techniques, the fact that the economic measures serving as central independent variables almost certainly include considerable error while the voting measures as dependent variables do not, means that the coefficients have been somewhat understated and the standard errors exaggerated. The extent of these distortions is difficult to determine, but their existence is especially likely in view of the tenuous quality of the investment dependence ratio, wherein some of the capital flows were of necessity estimated by interpolative procedures. The theoretical significance of this tendency toward conservatively small and unstable regression coefficients is simply that better data would yield somewhat closer fits to the compliance equations, although it is uncertain whether substantive interpretations would be significantly altered in the final analysis.

The second question about economic measures returns to the distinction between sensitivity dependence and vulnerability dependence. It is a country's vulnerability to asymmetrical economic ties, rather than its sensitivity, that is thought to provide its partner with political leverage. Thus, annual changes in trade, investment, and aid dependence may reveal more about short-term fluctuations in sensitivity than they do about latent long-term costs. Furthermore, this possibility of invalid measurement procedure seems most probable for those countries whose dependence scores do not show a secular change over the years. That is, fluctuations around a steady dependence on the U.S. are probably just sensitivity readings since they return in short order to a relatively unchanged level. This last point is conjectural, of course. But the broader possibility that annual change measures often tap shifts in sensitivity rather than in vulnerability threatens theoretical inferences based on the political economy hypotheses.

More specifically, this threat to measurement validity means that, insofar as vulnerability dependence is not captured by the change indicators, their associations with General Assembly voting scores cannot be expected to conform to the main compliance hypotheses. Vulnerability should produce compliance; sensitivity should not. Viewed in this light, rejecting the compliance hypotheses can be seen as confirmation of the interdependence proposition that economic sensitivity is not laden with political influence opportunity. Further, if the economic change indicators reflect sensitivity dependence, then this would also assist in resolving any remaining impression of contradictory findings between the two main empirical conclusions emerging from this study.

On the one hand, marked differences expected for Cold War voting patterns did in fact characterize the cross-sectional, grouped comparisons of dependencies and non-dependencies until the late 1960s, when the group averages began to converge. Yet, as the annual voting behavior of individual dependencies was regressed on their respective changes in economic dependence, the predicted associations seldom emerged. These two conclusions are not contradictory, since the first is a static comparison while the second is a longitudinal one. However, introducing the possibility that annual economic changes reflect sensitivity can resolve any lingering doubts regarding confusion between the first and second empirical results. To grasp this point, one needs to remember that the economic change data were only employed in the longitudinal tests. In contrast, the cross-sectional group comparisons singled out the dependent group of countries on the basis of their meeting a minimum dependence threshold with some consistency, a standard that suggests a condition of regular vulnerability quite apart from yearly changes in reliance on the U.S. economy. In short, the static comparisons offer a picture of group voting averages consistent with a generalized expectation of foreign policy compliance by vulnerable countries, but measures that may tap changes in sensitivity dependence show no patterned relationship to changes in voting agreement. Rather, voting shifts for dependent countries clearly tend to parallel those of nondependencies.

Finally, a secondary static comparison has suggested that western hemisphere countries, even those that have not qualified as dependencies, agree with the United States more often than do nonwestern countries, including four dependencies. Thus, even the cross-sectional evidence in favor of a compliance interpretation must at least be restricted to the hemisphere. And that inference is clouded, in turn, by the inclination of nondependent (or more correctly "semidependent") Latin countries to agree with the U.S. at a level about midway between their dependent neighbors and the rest of the world.

Policy Implications

Foreign policy officials and international business leaders can find many signs of change in relations between rich and poor countries. Host treatment of direct foreign investors is less generous than before. Poor countries are collectively pushing for a New International Economic Order.[9] And the predominant position of the United States in the capitalist markets has been eroding.

The decline of U.S. economic primacy relative to other industrial countries is well known. This deterioration is not only global, it has also been true of the U.S. presence in Latin America.[10] The hemispheric trend is reflected in the present research, where average economic dependence fell to an appreciably lower level in the last decade covered. Moreover, the fact that the dependence score for each country was weighted equally in computing the group average masks the fact that, among the dependencies, the larger economies have generally experienced decreasing dependence on the U.S. since the mid-1960s. The arithmetic compensations that gave a semblance of stability to the final decade derive from treating the dependence score of Trinidad and Tobago as equal in weight to that of, say, Colombia. In truth, however, the aggregate reliance of these twenty-three countries on the U.S. has continued to decline relative to their own collective size.

This does not signal an end to the external dependence of these poor countries. Rather, it mirrors the emergence of dependence ties to other industrialized economies. The dependencies remain greatly dependent on external provisions although not so exclusively reliant on the United States as they once were.

Two foreign policy implications stem from this diversification of dependence. First, officials in Washington should recognize that their potential economic leverage is diluted by the growing role of other industrial powers in Latin America, where the U.S. has long presumed a hegemonic position.[11] If the U.S. expects to be successful in its influence attempts, whether in the General Assembly or elsewhere, it is increasingly likely to find that "its" dependencies must balance Washington against Tokyo or Bonn. Second, the U.S. will probably encounter the same crosspressures operating within dependent societies. Its efforts to mobilize political support among local elites with vested interests in economic ties to the U.S. may now have to compete more frequently with other indigenous groups favoring economic bonds to other industrial centers.

The policies adopted by most poor countries have changed shape in recent years. National development is fully entrenched as a transcendent goal, but its pursuit is taking new forms. In foreign economic transactions, lessdeveloped countries are no longer content to suffer what they see as unfair disadvantages accruing to small units in an international market dominated by an industrial oligopoly. They have individually and collectively begun to demand a greater share of the benefits from foreign trade and investment. Furthermore, they have shown some willingness to assume the political risks that accompany their demands. However, by operating collectively in international organizations, they are minimizing their costs and perhaps even their risks.[12]

How will the U.S. respond? If, as suggested in the preceding discussion, the U.S. is simultaneously hampered by bargaining difficulties and regime changes that threaten to circumscribe the range of international issues on which it can retain a dominant force, the picture is disquieting for the superpower's decision-makers. Regardless of their personal reactions, they can surely sense that changes are afoot in at least certain facets of rich-poor relations. Further, most of them probably embrace (as an abstraction) the legitimacy of developmental aspirations that are so much a part of these changes.

Two opposing styles of response characterize the poles of a continuum of choice available to the United States. At one end of the spectrum lies massive resistance to change. Whether by threats of military force, subversion, or oligopolistic market leadership, the U.S. might undertake rear-guard actions in attempts to restore its unchallenged supremacy in the free world realized so fleetingly just after the second world war. To have any hope of success today, of course, the U.S. would have to accommodate its major Atlantic partners and Japan. With their assistance, the United States might attempt to resist commodity stabilization agreements, intervene diplomatically to protect foreign investors while holding out the threat of military action in the absence of satisfactory settlements, and use foreign aid as a political carrot. But such a path would lead to little success in any case; many of the strongest forces for change already elude U.S. control.[13]

This reactionary scenario may seem to be a fantasy; perhaps it is. But before it is dismissed too casually, it may be instructive to remember how quickly the Nixon administration tried to devalue General Assembly outcomes that were, by the early 1970s, so consistently leaving the U.S. in a minority voting coalition. Then-Ambassador John Scali decried the Assembly's "majority tyranny" dominated by the small and weak states. Granting that his remark was symbolic, it nevertheless suggested that Washington was inclined in at least one instance to deny change rather than to adjust to it.

The other extreme is a form of self-abnegation.[14] In this

scheme, the United States would not only embrace the idea of change, it would take all possible measures to assure that developed countries transfer needed developmental capital, materials, and skills to poor societies as rapidly as possible and free of charge; transfers would be limited only by the absorptive capacities of the recipients. Further, the U.S. would relinquish all authority to the recipients regarding the determination of their needs, except as asked to do otherwise. The limitless altruism embodied in this scenario takes it well beyond the limits of credulity.[15] Neither U.S. decision-makers nor their constituents are likely to come close to the requisite degree of sustained selflessness required for such an undertaking.

Relations between the U.S. and its dependencies must therefore follow policies falling somewhere between the futile search for the status quo ante and its opposite, the even less plausible extreme of unbounded self-abnegation. What choices will the U.S. make? The range of options between these poles is very great, and broad predictions, especially in a period of change, should be regarded with a heavy dose of circumspection.

Perhaps the safest prediction is that the United States will continue to experience great difficulty in developing a consistent and coordinated posture regardless of the general orientation that emerges. Efforts at consistency will probably be complicated by the phenomenon of issue separation with which U.S. policymakers are less familiar. For, not only must officials recognize that the great capabilities of the United States are rivaled by other industrial democracies, but they may also need to confront the prospect that, on certain issues, even the "weak" states may collectively be dominant participants; the general capabilities of the U.S. may not be applicable to those issue areas. Both observers and participants should hope that U.S. foreign policy somehow takes into account these complications. For only then can policy address issues with the clarity necessary for further adjustments to be made.

Conclusion

In concert with other investigations of asymmetrical interdependence and foreign policy, the theoretical inferences
and policy implications of this study are speculative but
suggestive. Scholars hope that as theory is refined and vali-
dated by additional systematic research, it becomes a more
potent resource for policymakers. This study indicates that
great U.S. economic advantages can no longer be used to
generate voting support in the General Assembly. Other
investigations suggest that the present findings fit into a
broader pattern: various types of superior capabilities face
mounting obstacles to their application as instruments of
influence. Disparities in national capabilities and asymmetries in international interdependence will presumably
persist in the foreseeable future. But the successful application of capabilities through channels of asymmetrical
relations seems to be increasingly issue-specific if not
uncertain.

Notes

1. Introduction

1. See Peter J. Katzenstein, "International Interdependence: Some Long-Term Trends and Recent Changes," *International Organization* 29, 4 (Autumn 1975), 1021–1034. Katzenstein concludes that the trend of decreasing transactions between the mid-1940s and the 1950s, discerned by Deutsch and others, has more recently undergone a reversal. One demonstration of the earlier downward trend is found in Karl W. Deutsch, Lewis J. Edinger, Roy C. Macridis, and Richard L. Merritt, *France, Germany and the Western Alliance* (New York: Charles Scribner's Sons, 1967), chap. 13.
2. Robert O. Keohane and Joseph S. Nye, *Power and Interdependence: World Politics in Transition* (Boston: Little Brown, 1977), p. 8.
3. See ibid., pp. 11–19.
4. Johan Galtung, "East-West Interaction Patterns," *Journal of Peace Research*, 1966 (no. 2), 146–177. For his application of this concept to economics between rich and poor countries, see Galtung, "A Structural Theory of Imperialism," *Journal of Peace Research*, 1971 (no. 2), 81–117. A strict interpretation of Galtung's conception is challenged by Jon A. Christopherson, "Structural Analysis of Transactions

Systems: Vertical Fusion or Network Complexity?"
Journal of Conflict Resolution 20, 4 (December
1976), 637–662. Using cross-sectional data for the
mid-1960s, Christopherson finds that foreign trade
patterns conform rather well to rank-dependent behavior predictions. However, patterns of diplomatic
visits are considerably more complex. The possibility that economic relations between rich and poor
countries are subject to change is explored in subsequent chapters.

5. There is debate about the effects of domestic economic
growth on the relative size of a country's foreign
economic activity. On the other hand, it is generally
agreed that small economies and nonindustrial
economies tend to be relatively more engaged in
external economic transactions. On these questions,
see Karl W. Deutsch and Alexander Eckstein, "National Industrialization and the Declining Share of
the International Economic Sector, 1890–1959,"
World Politics 13 (January 1961), 267–299; Katzenstein, "International Interdependence"; Kenneth
N. Waltz, "The Myth of National Interdependence," in *The International Corporation: A Sym-
posium*, ed. Charles P. Kindleberger (Cambridge,
Mass.: M.I.T. Press, 1970), especially pp. 213–
214; Richard Rosecrance and Arthur Stein, "Interdependence: Myth or Reality?" *World Politics* 26,
1 (October 1973), 1–27; Edward L. Morse, "Interdependence in World Affairs," in *World Politics:
An Introduction*, ed. James N. Rosenau, Kenneth
W. Thompson, and Gavin Boyd (New York: The
Free Press, 1976), pp. 660–681.

6. Galtung's "A Structural Theory of Imperialism" for-
malizes the idea of transnational elite alliances.

7. Theotonio Dos Santos, "The Structure of Dependence,"
in *Readings in U.S. Imperialism*, ed. K. T. Fann
and Donald C. Hodges (Boston: Porter Sargent,
1971), p. 226.

8. One could object to this distinction by arguing that political economy, by virtue of the interactive nature
of politics and economics, is not amenable to such

a division. However, granting that the identification of politics and economics as cause and effect may be an analytic artifice, it would appear to be at least equally as justifiable as any number of simplifying assumptions with which an inquiry into uncharted terrain might begin.

9. Donella H. Meadows, Dennis L. Meadows, Jørgen Randers, and William W. Behrens III, *The Limits to Growth* (New York: Universe Books, 1972).

10. The following points paraphrase Patrick J. McGowan and Klaus-Peter Gottwald, "Small State Foreign Policies: A Comparative Study of Participation, Conflict and Political and Economic Dependence in Black Africa," *International Studies Quarterly* 19, 4 (December 1975), 469–470.

2. International Economic Dependence

1. A more extensive array of categories, some as subsets of others, is created for *dependencia* ideas by Raymond Duvall et al., "A Formal Model of 'Dependencia' Theory: Structure, Measurement, and Some Preliminary Data," paper delivered at the International Political Science Association Congress, Edinburgh, Scotland, August 16–21, 1976.

2. Psychological aspects of dependence are considered in Chapter 3.

3. Albert O. Hirschman, *National Power and the Structure of Foreign Trade* (Berkeley: University of California Press, 1945). The theoretical presentation is found in his Chapter 2.

4. Ibid., p. 16.

5. Treatments of these theories are found in standard textbooks on international economics. See, for example, Charles P. Kindleberger, *International Economics*, 5th ed. (Homewood, Ill.: Richard D. Irwin, 1973), chaps. 2 and 3.

6. More correctly, pure trade theory predicts optimal efficiency ("pareto-optimality") only in the absence of monopolistic elements and barriers to trade, con-

ditions that are not met in actuality. The thesis developed in the following pages is that violations of trade theory systematically tend to penalize poor and small economies more than rich and larger ones as the former trade with the latter.

7. In much broader terms, Steven L. Spiegel emphasizes the same asymmetry of the stakes involved in *Dominance and Diversity: The International Hierarchy* (Boston: Little, Brown, 1972), p. 133.

8. One accounting, for example, puts the export earnings for poor countries at 80 percent of their foreign exchange, the remainder coming from private investment. See David H. Blake and Robert S. Walters, *The Politics of Global Economic Relations* (Englewood Cliffs, N.J.: Prentice-Hall, 1976), p. 127.

9. See D. K. Fieldhouse, *Economics and Empire 1830–1914* (Ithaca, N.Y.: Cornell University Press, 1973), p. 35.

10. See David Vital, *The Inequality of States* (London: Oxford University Press, 1967), chap. 3.

11. This conclusion about the dynamic effects of trade on domestic economic development gives greater weight to benefits of industrialization than to the possibility that economies of scale achieved by industrial exporters may also result in reduced prices for purchasers of their products, including consumers in nonindustrial countries.

12. "Terms of trade" in the context of dependence originates with the work of Raúl Prebisch. A good introduction to these ideas is his "Commercial Policy in the Underdeveloped Countries," *American Economic Review* 49, 2 (1959), 251–273. However, this thesis has come under strong attack by numerous economists on both empirical and theoretical grounds. For a useful overview of this controversy, and for further references, see C. Richard Bath and Dilmus D. James, "Dependency Analysis of Latin America: Some Criticisms, Some Suggestions," *Latin American Research Review* 11, 3 (Fall 1976), 6–7, 26–27. A dated, but good empirical survey is found in Alasdair MacBean, *Export*

Instability and Economic Development (Cambridge, Mass.: Harvard University Press, 1966), pp. 265–302.

13. See Richard N. Cooper, *The Economics of Interdependence: Economic Policy in the Atlantic Community* (New York: McGraw-Hill, 1968), p. 79. John Pincus, in *Trade, Aid and Development: The Rich Nations and the Poor Nations* (New York: McGraw-Hill, 1967), p. 328, regards price fluctuations as a minor concern far overshadowed by the chronic balance of payments problems of poor countries. Balance of payments are discussed in the next sections of this chapter.

14. See Albert O. Hirschman, *The Strategy of Economic Development* (New Haven: Yale University Press, 1958), pp. 110–119.

15. Galtung, "A Structural Theory of Imperialism," p. 87.

16. See Richard E. Caves and Ronald W. Jones, *World Trade and Payments: An Introduction* (Boston: Little, Brown, 1973), chap. 12.

17. See Vital, *Inequality of States*, chap. 3. The discussion here obviously refers to domestically owned industry, rather than to operations under foreign control.

18. See Helge Hveem, "The Global Dominance System: Notes on a Theory of Global Political Economy," *Journal of Peace Research*, 1973 (no. 4), 319–340.

19. Bela Balassa, *The Structure of Protection*, UNCTAD TD/B/C.2/36, 1970. The reader who is interested in the fact that effective tariffs are often higher than nominal rates of protection might consult Pincus, *Trade, Aid and Development*, pp. 189–194.

20. Harry Magdoff, *The Age of Imperialism* (New York: Monthly Review Press, 1969), p. 165.

21. J. M. Finger and A. I. Yeats, "Effective Protection by Transportation Costs and Tariffs: A Comparison of Magnitudes," *Quarterly Journal of Economics* 40, 1 (Feb. 1976), 169–176.

22. This rate is reported for the end of 1973 in U.S. Congress, Senate, Committee on Foreign Relations, Subcommittee on Multinational Corporations, *Direct*

Investment Abroad and the Multinationals: Effects on the United States Economy, prepared by Peggy B. Musgrave for 94th Cong., 1st sess. (Washington, D.C.: U.S. Government Printing Office, 1975), p. xi. The ratio remains unchanged through 1975 according to the time series shown in U.S. President, *International Economic Report of the President*, transmitted to the Congress January 1977 (Washington: U.S. Government Printing Office, 1977), Appendix B, p. 163, Table 46.

23. Blake and Walters, *The Politics of Global Economic Relations*, pp. 80–81.

24. The 1975 value for accumulated book value is taken from U.S. President, *Report of the President* (1977), p. 86, Figure 38. The annual average is calculated from the same source. Musgrave (*Direct Investment Abroad*, p. 1) reports a higher estimate "of the order of $140 billion" by the end of 1973. U.S. investment grew at the rate of 20 percent a year in the 1950s (see Musgrave, p. 11).

25. See Benjamin J. Cohen, *The Question of Imperialism: The Political Economy of Dominance and Dependence* (New York: Basic Books, 1973), pp. 158–159; Michael Barratt Brown, *The Economics of Imperialism* (Baltimore: Penguin Books, 1974), p. 207; Musgrave, *Direct Investment Abroad*, p. xi.

26. Robock and Simmonds, for example, put the U.S. share of accumulated world investment at over 55 percent in 1970. See Stefan H. Robock and Kenneth Simmonds, *International Business and Multinational Enterprise* (Homewood, Ill.: Richard D. Irwin, 1973), pp. 44–45.

27. F. H. Cardoso, "Dependency and Development in Latin America," *New Left Review* 74 (July–August 1972), sees a shift from one-third to two-thirds. However, Raymond Vernon shows with 1969 figures that about 70 percent of U.S. manufacturing investments in Latin America are located in just these three countries, where only 33 percent of

all U.S. investments in the region are hosted. (*Sovereignty at Bay: The Multinational Spread of U.S. Enterprises* [New York: Basic Books, 1971], p. 19). Vernon's report accords with Department of Commerce figures attributing to Argentina, Brazil, and Mexico 70 percent of the Latin American total in 1970 and 71 percent by 1974. See U.S. Department of Commerce, Bureau of Economic Analysis, *Revised Data Series on U.S. Direct Investment Abroad, 1966–1974* (Washington, D.C.: U.S. Government Printing Office, [n.d.]), pp. 5, 9, Tables 5 and 9.

28. Albert O. Hirschman, *How to Divest in Latin America, and Why*, Princeton Essays in International Finance, No. 76 (Princeton, N.J.: International Finance Section, 1969), p. 3.

29. See Cohen, *The Question of Imperialism*, p. 159. Another study estimates that some 83 percent of the finance capital for U.S. investment in Latin America is borrowed locally. See Richard J. Barnet and Ronald E. Müller, *Global Reach: The Power of the Multinational Corporations* (New York: Simon and Schuster, 1974), pp. 152–153. They cite Fernando Fajnzylber, *Estrategia Industrial y Empresas Internacionales: Posición relativa de América y Brasil* (Rio de Janeiro: United Nations, CEPAL, November 1970), p. 65.

30. See Herbert K. May, *The Contributions of U.S. Private Investment to Latin America's Growth* (New York: The Council for Latin America, 1970), p. 19. May found, for 1966, that U.S.-based multinational subsidiaries paid more than $1.5 billion in taxes to Latin American host governments, nearly 15 percent of those states' revenues.

31. These local interests are variously called "ad hoc allies" (Vital, *The Inequality of States*, chap. 3) and the "comprador" class (Barratt Brown, *Economics of Imperialism*, p. 277).

32. Cohen, *The Question of Imperialism*, p. 175. See also Vernon, *Sovereignty at Bay*, p. 173.

33. Vernon, *Sovereignty at Bay*, pp. 170–171.
34. Blake and Walters, *The Politics of Global Economic Relations*, p. 100.
35. Vernon, *Sovereignty at Bay*, p. 179.
36. See Blake and Walters, *The Politics of Global Economic Relations*, p. 99; Barnet and Müller, *Global Reach*, p. 157; Cohen, *The Question of Imperialism*, p. 158.
37. However, Vernon (*Sovereignty at Bay*, pp. 177–178) points out that counteractive local economic effects may erase this gain in the long run.
38. See ibid., pp. 175–176.
39. Ibid., p. 173.
40. Ibid., pp. 170–172.
41. See Galtung, "A Structural Theory of Imperialism."
42. Blake and Walters, *The Politics of Global Economic Relations*, p. 93.
43. See Miguel S. Wionczek, "United States Investment and the Development of Middle America," *Studies in Comparative International Development* 5, 2 (1969–1970), 3–17.
44. See Blake and Walters, *The Politics of Global Economic Relations*, p. 96, regarding the subsidiary's competitive advantage.
45. See Vernon, *Sovereignty at Bay*, pp. 181–186.
46. See Blake and Walters, *The Politics of Global Economic Relations*, pp. 96–97.
47. Ibid., p. 93. For a discussion of patent manipulation see Hveem, "The Global Dominance System."
48. Profit and certainty goals partially overlap with a third oft-mentioned objective, that of corporate growth. Agreeing with marxist critics about the attribution to multinationals of these capitalistic motives, Cohen adds: "If not they, then who?" (*The Question of Imperialism*, p. 203).
49. See Vernon, *Sovereignty at Bay*, p. 181.
50. An excellent overview is Albert O. Hirschman, "The Political Economy of Import-Substituting Industrialization in Latin America," *The Quarterly Journal of Economics* 82 (February 1968), 2–32.

51. Theodore Moran models the host's bargaining power in primary goods industries as an upward, ratcheted learning curve that permits the host government to renegotiate the contracts on successively more favorable terms over time. See *Multinational Corporations and the Politics of Dependence: Copper in Chile* (Princeton, N.J.: Princeton University Press, 1974), chap. 6.

52. Blake and Walters, *The Politics of Global Economic Relations*, pp. 125–126.

53. Vernon, *Sovereignty at Bay*, pp. 105–106.

54. See Economist Intelligence Unit, *The Growth and Spread of Multinational Companies*, rev. ed. (London: QER Special, 1971), p. 30.

55. See Moran, *Multinational Corporations and the Politics of Dependence*.

56. Musgrave, *Direct Investment Abroad*, pp. 12–13. These same 1100 largest U.S. firms claimed nearly half of all taxable domestic corporate income that year.

57. Jean-Jacques Servan-Schreiber's *The American Challenge* (New York: Atheneum, 1968) and Karl Levitt's *Silent Surrender: The American Economic Empire in Canada* (New York: Liveright, 1971) are probably the most widely cited examples of the parallel reactions often found in developed host societies.

58. Grants incur no debts; they are unilateral transfers. Concessional loans are those made on generous terms, for example, with interest rates below commercial levels and/or with grace periods before the first repayments are due to the lender.

59. Pincus (*Trade, Aid and Development*, p. 339) reports that multilateral aid grew from about 10 percent in the mid-1950s to 18 percent by 1964. It stood at nearly 28 percent by 1975 (see *Report of the President*, [1977], p. 171, Table 59).

60. Because most foreign aid is in the form of loans rather than grants, "donors" is a rather less appropriate designation than is "lenders." On the other hand,

> lenders are also donors when loans are made on generous terms. Hereafter, the two words will be used interchangeably.

61. Pincus, *Trade, Aid and Development*, p. 22.

62. See Edward S. Mason, "United States Interests in Foreign Economic Assistance," in *The United States and the Developing Economies*, ed. Gustav Ranis (New York: Norton, 1964), pp. 13–23; Eugene R. Wittkopf, "Containment Versus Underdevelopment in the Distribution of United States Foreign Aid: An Introduction to the Use of Crossnational Aggregate Data Analysis in the Study of Foreign Policy," in *Analyzing International Relations: A Multimethod Introduction*, ed. William D. Coplin and Charles W. Kegley, Jr. (New York: Praeger, 1975), pp. 80–93.

63. See Pincus, *Trade, Aid and Development*, p. 128, for the 1962 and 1970 figures, reported from OECD published data. The 1975 percentage is based on the *Report of the President* (1977). See Blake and Walters, *The Politics of Global Economic Relations*, pp. 129–132, for a brief review of reasons for the decline in U.S. foreign aid disbursement.

64. Gunnar Myrdal, *Economic Theory and Underdeveloped Regions* (New York: Duckworth, 1954), p. 339.

65. Cheryl Payer, *The Debt Trap: The International Monetary Fund and the Third World* (New York: Monthly Review Press, 1974), p. 29.

66. Bilateralism in trade may also be promoted by multilateral loans. Eugene Black, a former president of the World Bank, has been quoted as saying: "Our foreign aid programs constitute a distinct benefit to American business. . . . Foreign aid provides a substantial and immediate market for U.S. goods and services. . . . Foreign aid stimulates the development of new overseas markets for U.S. companies." Quoted in Magdoff, *The Age of Imperialism*, p. 176.

67. See Teresa Hayter, *Aid as Imperialism* (Baltimore: Penguin Books, 1971); and Payer, *The Debt Trap*.

68. Payer, *The Debt Trap*, pp. 217–218.
69. Ibid., p. 32.
70. Ibid., p. 33. Payer's commentary is less equivocal, asserting that these conditions are "standard" and "predictable."
71. Most of the following discussion is taken from ibid., pp. 33–42.
72. Ibid., p. 33.
73. Low local inflation decreases the risk factor perceived by potential foreign investors in that it suggests that the exchange rate will be stable, thereby making returns on investment predictable.
74. Blake and Walters, *The Politics of Global Economic Relations*, p. 134. Their data are taken from OECD, *Development Cooperation, 1973 Review*, pp. 67, 70.
75. J. H. Mensah in *The Guardian*, July 19, 1971 (quoted in Payer, *The Debt Trap*, p. 201).
76. Pincus, *Trade, Aid and Development*, p. 345.
77. Testimony to the importance of aid conditions to recipients' economic development is given in an AID discussion paper: "In the long run, aid's 'influence potential' is much more important than its resource contribution. This is true [in part because while] aid from all sources has probably contributed only roughly 20 percent of total investment in the developing countries [the accompanying policy reform conditions] are likely to have a greater impact on growth than the added capital and skills financed by aid." (G. Ranis and J. Nelson, *Measures to Ensure the Effective Use of Aid*, AID Discussion Paper No. 9, originally published in *Effective Aid*, ODI, 1966, p. 91. Quoted in Hayter, *Aid as Imperialism*, p. 89.)
78. See Hayter, *Aid as Imperialism*, pp. 158–162.
79. Ibid., p. 27. These effects, however, are not so likely if in fact inflation rates have declined as mentioned earlier.
80. Quoted in Payer, *The Debt Trap*, p. 31.
81. Ibid., pp. ix–x.
82. Hayter, *Aid as Imperialism*, p. 9 (emphasis added).

83. Payer, *The Debt Trap*, pp. 43–44.
84. Hayter, *Aid as Imperialism*, p. 15.
85. Pincus, *Trade, Aid and Development*, p. 311. It has often been suggested that donors are especially interested in securing access to raw materials. In this connection, see Gabriel Kolko, *The Roots of American Foreign Policy: An Analysis of Power and Purpose* (Boston: Beacon Press, 1969), chap. 3.
86. This effect assumes at least somewhat inelastic demand, a reasonable expectation for most unprocessed goods in particular.
87. Blake and Walters, *The Politics of Global Economic Relations*, p. 133; Hayter, *Aid as Imperialism*, p. 10.
88. Hayter, *Aid as Imperialism*, p. 158.
89. The balance of this paragraph paraphrases Payer, *The Debt Trap*, pp. 41–42.
90. It might also be argued that import liberalization destroys the shield behind which local producers previously enjoyed a protected market. However, currency devaluation may have offsetting effects since imports thereby become more expensive.
91. This sanction was apparently invoked by Secretary of State Rogers against the Chilean government of Salvador Allende. See Payer, *The Debt Trap*, pp. 190–194. On the other hand, the Hickenlooper Amendment was not used against Peru in its protracted dispute with the International Petroleum Company. The amendment has since been revoked.
92. Hayter, *Aid as Imperialism*, p. 15; Cohen, *The Question of Imperialism*, p. 199.
93. Payer, *The Debt Trap*, p. 214.
94. See Theotonio Dos Santos, "The Structure of Dependence," *American Economic Review* 60, 2 (May 1970); Stephen Hymer, "The Multinational Corporation and the Law of Uneven Development," in *Economics and World Order: From the 1970s to the 1990s*, ed. Jagdish N. Bhagwati (New York: Free Press, 1972), pp. 113–40; Duvall et al., "A Formal Model of 'Dependencia' Theory," especially p. 6, from which much of this discussion is taken.

3. Foreign Policy Compliance

1. This emphasis on relative costs and benefits between economics and politics is suggested by Karl W. Deutsch, *The Analysis of International Relations*, 2nd ed. (Englewood Cliffs, N.J.: Prentice-Hall, 1978), pp. 259–260.

2. See James N. Rosenau, "Pre-Theories and Theories of Foreign Policy," in *Approaches to Comparative and International Politics*, ed. R. Barry Farrell (Evanston, Ill.: Northwestern University Press, 1966), pp. 27–92, where he discusses the "penetration" of one society by another. His "linkage" ideas are laid out in "Introduction: Political Science in a Shrinking World," in *Linkage Politics: Essays on the Convergence of National and International Systems*, ed. James N. Rosenau (New York: Free Press, 1969), pp. 1–17; "Toward the Study of National-International Linkages," in *Linkage Politics*, pp. 44–63; "Theorizing Across Systems: Linkage Politics Revisited," in *Conflict Behavior and Linkage Politics*, ed. Jonathan Wilkenfeld (New York: David McKay, 1973), pp. 25–56.

3. For a brief critique of Rosenau's "linkage politics" framework in the context of global interdependence, see Ralph Pettman, *Human Behavior and World Politics: An Introduction to International Relations* (New York: St. Martin's, 1975), pp. 40–47.

4. James N. Rosenau, *The Adaptation of National Societies* (New York: General Learning Press, 1970); and "Foreign Policy as Adaptive Behavior," *Comparative Politics* 2 (April 1970), 365–387.

5. Melvin Gurtov, *The United States against the Third World: Antinationalism and Intervention* (New York: Praeger, 1974), p. 205. Also see the note on p. 202, where Gurtov concludes that U.S. policy toward the Third World has generally been motivated by the desire "to preserve or expand *dependency relationships* . . . by insuring access to, and exerting predominant influence over, their politics,

economies, and military affairs."

6. *New York Times,* October 27, 1971, p. 16, as reported by Eugene R. Wittkopf, "Foreign Aid and United Nations Votes: A Comparative Study," *American Political Science Review* 67, 3 (September 1973), 868.

7. Osvaldo Sunkel, "Commentary on Pinto," in *Latin America and the United States: The Changing Political Realities,* ed. Julio Cotler and Richard R. Fagen (Stanford, California: Stanford University Press, 1974), p. 126.

8. See *Group Dynamics: Research and Theory,* ed. Dorwin Cartwright and Alvin Zander (New York: Harper & Row, 1968), p. 230.

9. Social psychologists refer to such behavior as "conformity" or "compliance." See Herbert C. Kelman, "Compliance, Identification, and Internalization: Three Processes of Attitude Change," *Journal of Conflict Resolution* 2 (1958), 51–60. Kelman's compliance and conformity as overt behavior styles correspond to the expectations here. But they do not require "internalization," behavior motivated by the intrinsic rewards of the acts for the actor.

10. The rank-dependent framework was summarized in Chapter 1.

11. I have conducted partial tests of this proposition in two earlier studies. See my "Political Compliance and U.S. Trade Dominance," *American Political Science Review* 70, 4 (December 1976), 1098–1109, for a cross-sectional investigation. A later project is reported in a study conducted with Charles W. Kegley, Jr., "International Economic Dependence and Political Compliance: A Longitudinal Analysis," paper delivered at the annual meeting of the International Studies Association, St. Louis, Missouri, March 16–20, 1977. Also related by their implicit linearity propositions are the following empirical studies of economic dependence and foreign policy behavior: Marshall R. Singer and Barton Sensenig III, "Elections within the United Na-

tions," *International Organization* 17, 3 (Autumn 1963), 901–925; Wittkopf, "Foreign Aid and United Nations Votes," pp. 868–888; James T. Bennett and Miguel A. Guzman, "Political Allegiance as a Determinant of Multilateral Aid in Latin America," in *The Politics of Aid, Trade, and Investment*, ed. Satish Raichur and Craig Liske (New York: John Wiley & Sons, Halsted Press, 1976), pp. 87–94.

12. Vital, *Inequality of States*, p. 90.
13. Spiegel, *Dominance and Diversity*, p. 19.
14. Ibid., p. 142.
15. Galtung, "A Structural Theory of Imperialism."
16. Susanne Bodenheimer, "Dependency and Imperialism: The Roots of Latin American Underdevelopment," in *Readings in U.S. Imperialism*, ed. Fann and Hodges, pp. 163–164. The passage she quotes is from Paul Baran, *The Political Economy of Growth* (New York: Monthly Review Press, 1957), pp. 194–195.
17. Marshall R. Singer, *Weak States in a World of Powers: The Dynamics of International Relationships* (New York: Free Press, 1972), pp. 226–227. The choice by elites in a dependency to pursue private gain rather than public good, insofar as the two can be distinguished, has been suggested as an indication of "exploitation" by Moran (*Multinational Corporations and the Politics of Dependence*, pp. 155–156, 195–196). In contrast, James Caporaso suggests very different measurement criteria in "Methodological Issues in the Measurement of Inequality, Dependence, and Exploitation," in *Testing Theories of Economic Imperialism*, ed. Steven J. Rosen and James R. Kurth (Lexington, Mass.: Lexington Books, 1974), pp. 87–114.
18. Singer, *Weak States in a World of Powers*, p. 224. This same association between domestic economic and political interests is also assumed by Deutsch and Eckstein, "National Industrialization and the Declining Share of the International Economic Sec-

tor, 1890–1959," and by Robert T. Holt and John E. Turner, "Insular Polities," in *Linkage Politics*, ed. Rosenau, pp. 147–195.

19. McGowan and Gottwald, "Small State Foreign Policies," p. 471. Their first references are to Rosenau's "Pre-Theories and Theories of Foreign Policy" and *Linkage Politics*. The second set of references is to Ali A. Mazrui, *On Heroes and Uhuru-Worship: Essays on Independent Africa* (London: Longmans, 1967); Mazrui, *Towards a Pax Africana: A Study of Ideology and Ambition* (London: Weidenfeld & Nicolson, 1967); V. McKay, ed., *African Diplomacy* (New York: Praeger, 1966). The same position is echoed in Bruce M. Russett's reflections on some of his landmark investigations (with Hayward Alker) into United Nations voting behavior: "Votes on smaller, more parochial, and more transient issues are of course more difficult to predict. But on [the] continuing and salient cleavages we could do very well at the aggregate, macroscopic level without knowing anything about changing conditions or decision-processes *within* individual governments. Changes of personnel in the delegations; changes in the leadership of home governments; alternation of parties [in power]; all had little effect." ("A Macroscopic View of International Politics," in *The Analysis of International Politics: Essays in Honor of Harold and Margaret Sprout*, ed. James N. Rosenau, Vincent Davis, and Maurice A. East [New York: Free Press, 1972], p. 114.)

20. "UP Program of Government," *New Chile*, prepared and edited by the North American Congress on Latin America [NACLA] (New York: 1972), pp. 141–142, as quoted by Octavio Ianni, "Imperialism and Diplomacy in Inter-American Relations," in *Latin America and the United States*, ed. Cotler and Fagen, p. 37.

21. Moran, *Multinational Corporations and the Politics of Dependence*, pp. 6, 4.

22. Raymond Vernon, Letter to the Editor, *New York Times*, November 18, 1963, p. 32.

23. Spiegel, *Dominance and Diversity*, p. 144.

24. See Jack Nagel, "Inequality and Discontent: A Nonlinear Hypothesis," *World Politics* 26, 4 (July 1974), 453–472, for the development and application of such a construct to the proposition that inequalities among groups within societies are related to social turmoil within those countries.

25. Spiegel, *Dominance and Diversity*, pp. 120–121.

26. Karl W. Deutsch, "Social Mobilization and Political Development," *American Political Science Review* 55, 3 (September 1961), 493. This discussion owes significantly to Moran, *Multinational Corporations and the Politics of Dependence*, pp. 219–220.

27. The term "privileged problems" is developed by Albert O. Hirschman, *Journeys toward Progress* (New York: Doubleday, 1965).

28. See Chapter 2. Also see Andrew Mack, "Comparing Theories of Economic Imperialism," in *Testing Theories of Economic Imperialism*, ed. Rosen and Kurth, pp. 38–39.

29. See Moran, *Multinational Corporations and the Politics of Dependence*, p. 221. Recall that foreign investors may serve as a "lightning rod" for resentment (see Chapter 2 above).

30. Abraham F. Lowenthal, "The United States and Latin America: Ending the Hegemonic Presumption," *Foreign Affairs* 55, 1 (October 1976), 210.

31. See Hayward R. Alker, Jr., and Bruce M. Russett, *World Politics in the General Assembly* (New Haven: Yale University Press, 1965), for evidence that East-West issues were of growing importance over the first fifteen years of the U.N.'s existence.

32. Graham T. Allison, "Conceptual Models and the Cuban Missile Crisis," *American Political Science Review* 63, 3 (September 1969), 689–718; *Essence of Decision: Explaining the Cuban Missile Crisis* (Boston: Little, Brown, 1971).

33. See Robert Axelrod, "Bureaucratic Decisionmaking in

the Military Assistance Program: Some Empirical Findings," in *Readings in American Foreign Policy: A Bureaucratic Perspective*, ed. Morton H. Halperin and Arnold Kanter (Boston: Little, Brown, 1973), pp. 163–166.

34. Cybernetics emphasizes that information provided by feedback from an initial action would, in turn, better inform a second decision. Accordingly, equivocal decisions are desirable in the face of uncertainty. See Karl W. Deutsch, *The Nerves of Government: Models of Political Communication and Control* (New York: Free Press, 1966).

35. Charles E. Lindblom summarizes strategies of caution and incrementalism in *The Policy-Making Process* (Englewood Cliffs, N.J.: Prentice-Hall, 1968), chap. 4.

36. Bruce M. Russett, *International Regions and the International System: A Study in Political Ecology* (Chicago: Rand McNally, 1967). His first chapter succinctly reviews the controversies surrounding the matter of international regions.

37. Ibid., chap. 2. The label "Catholic culture" refers to the highly intercorrelated variables of (1) Catholics as a percentage of the population, (2) Christians as a percentage, (3) votes for socialist parties as a percentage, and some other moderately associated cultural variables. "Economic development" refers to (1) GNP per capita, (2) newspapers and (3) radios per capita, (4) life expectancy, (5) percentage of labor force in industry, (6) pupils in primary and secondary schools, (7) urbanization, (8) physicians per capita, and the like.

38. Ibid., chaps. 5 and 6.

39. Alker and Russett, *World Politics in the General Assembly*.

40. Ibid., chap. 12.

41. Ibid., p. 266. Prominent among issues that aligned delegates on an "East-West" basis were cold war and colonialism questions.

42. Alker and Russett found that neither trade with the U.S. nor aid received from it was significantly cor-

related with voting deviance within the Latin American group (ibid., pp. 258–259).

4. U.S. Economic Dependencies

1. Patrick J. McGowan, "Economic Dependence and Economic Performance in Black Africa," *Journal of Modern African Studies* 14, 1 (1976), 36.
2. See, for example, Russett, *International Regions and the International System*, chap. 8; Marshall R. Singer, *Weak States in a World of Powers: The Dynamics of International Relationships* (New York: Free Press, 1972), chap. 6.
3. A substantially different measure, "relative acceptance," was developed by Richard I. Savage and Karl W. Deutsch, "A Statistical Model of the Gross Analysis of Transaction Flows," *Econometrica* 28 (July 1960), 551–572. However, Cal Clark and Susan Welch present reasons for preferring a measure that divides trade by GNP in studies such as the present one. See their "Western European Trade as a Measure of Integration: Untangling the Interpretations," *Journal of Conflict Resolution* 16 (September 1972), especially 337.
4. See Deutsch and Eckstein, "National Industrialization," p. 274; Singer, *Weak States in a World of Powers*, pp. 248, 256; Masakatsu Sato, "A Model of U.S. Foreign Aid Allocation: An Application of a Rational Decision-Making Scheme," in *Approaches to Measurement in International Relations: A Non-Evangelical Survey*, ed. John E. Mueller (New York: Appleton-Century-Crofts, 1969), pp. 198–215.
5. Michael Michaely, "Concentration of Exports and Imports: An International Comparsion," *Economic Journal* 68, no. 272 (December 1958), 727.
6. United Nations, Statistical Office, *Yearbook of International Trade Statistics* (New York: various years, 1951–1974). Other sources are International Monetary Fund/International Bank for Reconstruction

and Development, *Direction of Trade* (Washington, D.C.: various years); René Codoni et al., *World Trade Flows: Integrational Structure and Conditional Forecasts*, vol. 2 (Statistical Appendix) (Zurich: Center for Economic Research, Swiss Federal Institute of Technology, 1971); U.S. Department of Commerce, Bureau of Foreign Commerce, *Economic Reports* (Washington: various issues beginning in 1954).

7. United Nations, Statistical Office, *Yearbook of National Accounts Statistics* (New York: various years 1957–1975); United States Arms Control and Disarmament Agency, *World Military Expenditures and Arms Trades, 1963–1973* (Washington, D.C.: 1975). Supplementary GNP data, including estimates based on parallel series of gross domestic product or national income figures, are from International Monetary Fund, *International Financial Statistics*, vol. 22 and Annual 1967/1968 (Washington, D.C.); and United Nations, Statistical Office, *Statistical Yearbook* (New York: various years), many of which are reported in Codoni et al., *World Trade Flows*; International Bank for Reconstruction and Development, *Trends in Developing Countries* (Washington, D.C.: 1971); Latin American Center, *Statistical Abstract of Latin America* (Los Angeles: University of California at Los Angeles, various years).

8. *Survey of Current Business* (Washington, D.C.: 1951–1976, various issues); *United States Balance of Payments, Statistical Supplement*, rev. ed., 1963; ~~Revised Data Series on U.S. Direct Investment~~ *Abroad, 1966–1974*, all published by the United States Department of Commerce, and the latter graciously made available to me by George Kruer of the Bureau of Economic Analysis at the Department of Commerce. Duplicate and additional U.S. investment values come from United Nations, Economic Commission for Latin America, *Economic Survey of Latin America: 1970* (New York: United Nations, 1972), p. 103; OECD, Development As-

sistance Directorate, *Stock of Private Direct Invest-*
ments by D.A.C. Countries in Developing Countries
end 1967 (Paris: OECD, 1972); Gert Rosenthal,
"The Role of Private Foreign Investment in the
Development of the Central American Common
Market," 2nd rev. (mimeographed: May/June
1974); U.S. Congress, Joint Economic Committee,
Private Investment in Latin America: Hearings be-
fore the Subcommittee on Inter-American Econom-
ic Relationships of the Joint Economic Committee,
88th Cong., 2nd sess., January 1964, pp. 51, 450;
Peter Drysdale, ed., *Direct Foreign Investment in*
Asia and the Pacific (Toronto: University of To-
ronto Press, 1972), pp. 248, 273, 321; United Na-
tions, Department of Economic and Social Affairs,
Foreign Capital in Latin America, Statistical Appendix (New York: United Nations, 1955), p. 159;
Felipe Pazos, "Private versus Public Foreign Investment in Under-developed Areas," in *Economic*
Development for Latin America, ed. Howard S.
Ellis (London: Macmillan, 1961), p. 204.

Changes in total (world) foreign investments,
discussed below, are from United Nations, Economic Commission for Latin America, *Economic Bulle-*
tin for Latin America 17, 1 (1972), 106; United
Nations, Economic Commission for Latin America,
Economic Survey of Latin America: 1964, p. 279.
Additional U.S. percentage shares of total investment are from U.N., ELCA, *Economic Survey*
(1970); OECD, *Stock of Private Direct Investments*.
9. For some countries, it is necessary to use gross fixed
capital formation as a close approximation.
10. (Washington, D.C.: IMF, Dec. 1959–May 1977). For
Brazil and Ecuador, exchange rates are taken from
U.S. Department of Commerce, Commerce Committee for the Alliance for Progress, *Proposals to*
Improve the Flow of U.S. Private Investment to
Latin America (Washington, D.C.: 1963), Appendix A, p. 4. In five cases, domestic capital formation in the last few years has been estimated on
the basis of parallel series reported under the re-

vised United Nations System of National Accounts (SNA). Finally, capital formation for Brazil is based on the revised SNA for 1970 through 1973.

11. Two published sources giving the annual figures for 1958 through 1973 are used. They are AID, Statistics and Reports Division, *U.S. Overseas Loans and Grants and Assistance from International Organizations: Obligations and Loan Authorizations July 1, 1945–June 30, 1967* (Washington, D.C.: 1968); and, with the same main title, *Obligations and Loan Authorizations July 1, 1945–June 30, 1974* (Washington, D.C.: n.d.).

12. I am grateful for the assistance provided by Carole Woodward of the AID staff in preparing these figures for this study.

13. Singer, *Weak States in a World of Powers*, pp. 237–240. Also see my "Political Compliance," pp. 1104–1105 and p. 1102, note 19.

14. Actually, 14.6 is used in order to accommodate rounding.

15. Trinidad and Tobago and Liberia, although the Liberian data set is incomplete.

16. The Philippines is dependent in only nine of the twenty-four years, and Venezuela is dependent in only ten, but both countries fall just short of the threshold in several other years.

17. "Inequality" and other appropriate measurement strategies are usefully discussed in Caporaso, "Methodological Issues in the Measurement of Inequality, Dependence, and Exploitation," pp. 87–114.

18. For example, see André Gunder Frank, *Capitalism and Underdevelopment in Latin America: Historical Studies of Chile and Brazil* (New York: Monthly Review Press, 1967).

19. These remarks are based on figures given in Charles Lewis Taylor and Michael C. Hudson, *World Handbook of Political and Social Indicators*, 2nd ed. (New Haven: Yale University Press, 1972), pp. 306–321.

20. Their summary dependence scores over all years aver-

age as follows: Argentina, 3.6; Brazil, 9.6; Mexico, 9.8.

21. If one were to compute dependence scores for all countries in the world, the result might approximate a normal distribution, of which these twenty-three dependencies would constitute the "most dependent" tail. Thus, both the high variance as well as the clustering of scores between 15 and 20 may not come as a surprise.

22. One contributor to this decline may be the increased private borrowing of many poor countries, especially in the 1970s, a capital movement not included in this dependence measure.

23. However, there is a tendency for shorter time series to yield higher coefficients as a statistical artifact.

24. In the case of Chile, of course, the reduction after 1969 was substantially a U.S. decision to pressure the Allende government, rather than a demonstration that a dependent economy can move away from dependence of its own volition.

25. David Ray refers to the assumption that dependence and dependent countries are homogeneous as a basic flaw in much of the *dependencia* literature. See his "The Dependency Model of Latin American Underdevelopment: Three Basic Fallacies," *Journal of Inter-American Studies and World Affairs* 15 (1973), 4–20.

26. See I. William Zartman, "Europe and Africa: Decolonization or Dependency?" *Foreign Affairs* 54, 2 (January 1976), 325–343.

27. Recent cross-national investigations include L. R. Alschuler, "Satellization and Stagnation in Latin America," *International Studies Quarterly* 20 (1976), 39–82; C. Chase-Dunn, "The Effect of International Economic Dependence on Development and Inequality: A Cross-National Study," *American Sociological Review* 40 (1975), 720–738; R. Kaufman, D. S. Geller, and H. T. Chernotsky, "A Preliminary Test of Dependency," *Comparative Politics* 7 (1975), 303–330; James Lee Ray and Thomas Webster, "Dependency and Economic Per-

formance in Latin America," *International Studies Quarterly* 22, 3 (September 1978).

5. Compliance in the General Assembly

1. A similar argument is found in Russett, *International Regions and the International System*, chap. 4, especially p. 60. In addition to voting data such as those used in this study, the growing body of events data created by students of comparative foreign policy behavior stands out as a second exception to the statement that there is no satisfactory evidence available. A recent digest of the problems and progress of events data collection and analysis is Charles W. Kegley, Jr., et al., eds., *International Events and the Comparative Analysis of Foreign Policy* (Columbia, S.C.: University of South Carolina Press, 1975). An important drawback of events data in the present context is their coverage of only a relatively short period of years.

2. This paraphrases David Truman, *The Congressional Party* (New York: John Wiley & Sons, 1959), p. 13, quoted in Alker and Russett, *World Politics in the General Assembly*, p. 23. For a similar justification, see Thomas Hovet, *Bloc Politics in the United Nations* (Cambridge: Harvard University Press, 1960), p. 113. K. B. Rai concludes that "voting in the U.N. G[eneral] A[ssembly] is a direct expression of national foreign policy." See "Foreign Policy and Voting in the United Nations General Assembly," *International Organization* 26, 3 (Summer 1972), 587. On the other hand, Eugene Wittkopf summarizes the most important criticisms of United Nations roll call data in his "Soviet and American Political Success in the United Nations General Assembly, 1946–70," in *International Events*, ed. Kegley et al., p. 179. Then, on the following page, he discusses some of the virtues of the data.

3. Inis L. Claude, *The Changing United Nations* (New

York: Random House, 1967), p. 53. Case study evidence is offered by John G. Stoessinger, *The United Nations and the Superpowers* (New York: Random House, 1965).

4. Robert O. Keohane, "Political Influence in the General Assembly," *International Conciliation*, no. 557 (March 1966), p. 19. Some support to this proposition is offered by a study by Eugene R. Wittkopf, who found a discernible positive association between U.S. foreign aid allocation and its recipients' Assembly and committee agreement with the donor in 1963 and 1966. See his "Foreign Aid and United Nations Votes," pp. 868–888. Singer and Sensenig discovered that nations' economic, military, perceptual, and communications ties with the superpowers were associated with paired voting agreement on cold war questions from 1946 to 1959. See their "Elections within the United Nations," pp. 901–925. As Singer phrased it elsewhere, "the way a country votes in international organizations on political issues of major concern to the mentor Powers" may be a sensitive indicator of political influence and compliance. In such an arena, "some weaker associated states tend to support their mentors more than others in those organizations" (*Weak States in a World of Powers*, pp. 323, 325). Also see note 11 in Chapter 2, above.

5. See Michael K. O'Leary, "Linkages between Domestic and International Politics in Underdeveloped Nations," in *Linkage Politics*, ed. Rosenau, p. 344.

6. See George L. Reid, *The Impact of Very Small Size on the International Behavior of Microstates*, Sage Professional Papers in International Studies, vol. 2 (Beverly Hills: Sage Publications, 1974), pp. 30–31.

7. Karl W. Deutsch, *The Analysis of International Relations* (Englewood Cliffs, N.J.: Prentice-Hall, 1968), pp. 24–25. Also see T. Baumgartner and T. R. Burns, "The Structuring of International Economic Relations," *International Studies Quarterly* 19, 2 (June 1975), 134.

8. Arend Lijphart, "The Analysis of Bloc Voting in the General Assembly," *American Political Science Review* 57, 4 (December 1963), 910. His index is divided by 100 here to achieve comparability with other measures.

9. The same argument to the effect that a country restricts its influence attempts to salient issues is made explicitly in William D. Coplin et al., *American Foreign Policy* (North Scituate, Mass.: Duxbury, 1974), p. 14.

10. Alker and Russett (*World Politics in the General Assembly*, chap. 10) measure nations' issue "intensities" by the number of speeches made by their delegates in the Assembly. They find that the United States and the Soviet Union were increasingly intense regarding their "East-West" confrontations through the 1961 session, the last they examined.

11. U.S. Congress, Senate, Committee on Foreign Relations, Subcommittee on Multinational Corporations, *Multinational Corporations and United States Foreign Policy*, 93rd Cong., 1st sess. (Washington: U.S. Government Printing Office, 1973), Part II, pp. 542–543.

12. Alternative means of operationalizing "Cold War" voting are reviewed in my "Political Compliance and U.S. Trade Dominance," p. 1104, note 4. On the broader utility of partitioning roll calls to measure success, see E. T. Rowe, "Changing Patterns in the Voting Success of Member States in the United Nations General Assembly: 1945–1966," *International Organization* 23, 2 (Spring 1969), 231–253.

13. This is a frequent practice. See Alker and Russett, *World Politics in the General Assembly*; Lijphart, "Analysis of Bloc Voting in the General Assembly," p. 910. Absences are not coded. Following John E. Mueller, a delegate's absence is not counted whenever it seems due to "reasons which are best attributed to apathy or disinterest" (*Approaches to Measurement in International Relations*, p. 139). For similar reasons, those delegates present but not voting are not included in the data.

14. "United Nations Roll Calls: Plenary Meetings of the General Assembly," vol. 1 (1967) and supplements. The roll call data were originally collected by Charles Wrigley. Neither the original collector of the data nor the Consortium bears any responsibility for the analyses or interpretations presented here.

15. As discussed in Chapter 4, Jordan, Nepal, Thailand, and Uganda might well have been included as dependencies if more economic data were available. Accordingly, they have not been included as nondependent countries for any of the statistical comparisons reported in this study.

16. Owing to the U.N.'s financial crisis, the General Assembly met but did not vote in 1964.

17. Eugene Wittkopf, using a different measurement procedure, also finds support for the U.S. to have declined. In fact, his technique leads to the conclusion that the waning fortunes of the U.S. began in the U.N.'s third session (1949). See his "Soviet and American Political Success."

18. References to estimates and true values follow convention to the effect that this study samples from a population of similar observations from years other than those examined.

19. For a summary statement of the effects of error distributions in correlation and regression statistics, see Mordecai Ezekiel and Karl A. Fox, *Methods of Correlation and Regression Analysis: Linear and Curvilinear*, 3rd ed. (New York: John Wiley & Sons, 1959), p. 312.

20. The multiplicative version takes the form $\Delta IA_t = [IA_1^{\ln(a)}] [D_{t-1}^{\ln(b)}]$.

21. Here, the length of the series is already stretched by using only export and aid dependence ratios.

22. Outliers may, of course, also deflate coefficients for other dependencies, particularly those others with relatively short time series.

23. This logic also explains why it makes no sense to add together all countries in a single test of the hypothesis.

24. For example, a statistical transformation can permit the parabolic expectation to be estimated by a linear regression equation, as illustrated in Nagel's "Inequality and Discontent," pp. 458–459.

25. Additionally, an outlying observation for Liberia again produces a supportive (parabolic) result statistically but not substantively.

26. The 1973 year-end book values are from U.S. Department of Commerce, *Revised Data Series*, p. 8, Table 8.

27. This 1973 figure presumably continues to reflect the very sizable holdings of the International Petroleum Corporation, a subsidiary of Standard Oil of New Jersey (now Exxon), in dispute with the government in Lima since 1969.

28. Bivariate correlations among the independent variables are quite low, indicating that it is safe to interpret the coefficients straightforwardly.

29. I am indebted to Stuart Bremer for bringing this point to my attention.

30. They are Barbados (voting since 1967), Mexico (beginning in 1960, when it is no longer economically dependent on the U.S.), Brazil (beginning in 1962, for the same reason as Mexico), Argentina, and Uruguay.

31. Kenneth E. Boulding, "National Images and International Systems," *Journal of Conflict Resolution* 3, 2 (June 1959), 130.

6. Theoretical and Policy Implications

1. Keohane and Nye, *Power and Interdependence*, p. 19.

2. Ibid., chaps. 1–3, on which much of the following discussion is based.

3. Ibid., p. 11.

4. Ibid., pp. 18–19. Also see the case study interpretations in their Chapter 7.

5. Ibid., pp. 49–52.

6. Evidence of the linkage between international economic ties and cold war politics, as perceived by the U.S.,

is indicated in Chapters 2 and 3 of this study.

7. "High politics" was coined by Stanley Hoffman in an analysis of Western European integration and Atlantic relations. See his "Obstinate or Obsolete? The Fate of the Nation-State and Case of Western Europe," *Daedalus* 95, 3 (Summer 1966).

8. Conflicts between foreign investors and relevant host elites have been reported by Moran (*Multinational Corporations*) and Franklin Tugwell (*The Politics of Oil in Venezuela*. [Stanford, Calif.: Stanford University Press, 1975]). Disputes between officials of the Inter-American Development Bank and Colombian development planners (with the Colombians prevailing) are documented by Gabriel Murillo's and Elizabeth Ungar's case study, "Programa Integrado de Desarrollo Urbano de la Zona Oriental de Bogotá (PIDUZOB)," in *Poder e Información*, ed. Edgar Revéiz (Bogotá, Colombia: El Centro de Estudios sobre Desarrollo Económico, 1977), pp. 249–342.

9. The objectives of the New International Economic Order (NIEO) are much more comprehensive than the trade reform goals initially set by UNCTAD in the 1960s. The formal NIEO provisions are spelled out in "Declaration on the Establishment of a New International Economic Order," Resolutions adopted by the General Assembly of the United Nations during the Sixth Special Session, May (1974). The political economy of the proposals embodied in these resolutions is widely discussed. A representative selection of topics and viewpoints is found in *The New International Economic Order: The North-South Debate*, ed. Jagdish N. Bhagwati (Cambridge, Mass.: M.I.T. Press, 1977).

10. Lowenthal provides a useful synopsis of this trend and discusses some of its implications for future U.S. foreign policy. See his "The United States and Latin America."

11. This is Lowenthal's (ibid.) main theme.

12. See Keohane and Nye, *Power and Interdependence*, p. 31. The risks may of course include those that the

present study has identified with their faliure to comply with U.S. preferences on Cold War votes, although earlier in this chapter it is suggested that perhaps the U.S. no longer perceives General Assembly matters of any kind as very important.

13. Albert O. Hirschman makes an interesting argument to the effect that policies designed to preserve the status quo are often self-defeating. Not only do such policies have unintended consequences that may promote change, but resultant changes are unexpected and therefore many times unnoticed until they are well established. See his "Introduction: Political Economics and Possibilism," in *A Bias for Hope: Essays on Development and Latin America* (New Haven: Yale University Press, 1971), pp. 35–37.

14. Self-abnegation as one of three foreign policy styles is discussed in Arnold Wolfers, "The Pole of Power and the Pole of Indifference," *World Politics* 4 (1951), 39–63.

15. Hirschman has suggested some less drastic and hence more plausible modes for increasing the transfer of resources to poor countries. See *A Bias for Hope*, pp. 28–29.

Index